FROM THE SCHOLAR TO THE CLASSROOM

Translating Jewish Tradition into Curriculum

FROM THE SCHOLAR TO THE CLASSROOM

Translating Jewish Tradition into Curriculum

Edited by
Seymour Fox
and
Geraldine Rosenfield

Melton Research Center for Jewish Education
THE JEWISH THEOLOGICAL SEMINARY OF AMERICA

CONTENTS

CONFEREES

Participants in Conference on Applying Jewish Scholarship to Contemporary Programs of Education, held January 8-10, 1973 at The Ohio State University under the sponsorship of the Melton Research Center for Jewish Education of The Jewish Theological Seminary of America and the Jewish Studies Program of The Ohio State University. (Academic identification as of January 1973.)

WALTER I. ACKERMAN
Professor of Education and Vice President for Academic Affairs, University of Judaism (On Leave); Chairman, Department of Education, and Dean of Faculties of Humanities and Social Sciences, Ben Gurion University of the Negev, Beer Sheva.

ROBERT ALTER
Professor of Comparative Literature, University of California, Berkeley.

ARNOLD BAND
Department of Near Eastern Studies, University of California, Los Angeles.

ROBERT L. CHAZAN
Melton Associate Professor of Jewish History and Studies, The Ohio State University.

BURTON I. COHEN
Assistant Professor in Education and National Director of Ramah Camps, The Jewish Theological Seminary of America.

GERSON D. COHEN
Chancellor and Jacob H. Schiff Professor in Jewish History, The Jewish Theological Seminary of America.

CHARLES CUTTER
Jewish studies bibliographer, The Ohio State University.

ELLIOT DORFF
> Director of Graduate Studies and Assistant Professor of Philosophy, University of Judaism, Los Angeles.

SYLVIA ETTENBERG
> Associate Dean, Seminary College - Teachers Institute, The Jewish Theological Seminary of America.

LOUIS FINKELSTEIN
> Chancellor Emeritus and Solomon Schechter Professor in Theology, The Jewish Theological Seminary of America.

JUNE FOX
> Assistant Professor of Education, The Ohio State University.

MARVIN FOX
> Appleman Professor of Jewish Thought, Brandeis University; Yassenoff Professor of Philosophy and Jewish Studies, The Ohio State University.

SEYMOUR FOX
> Director and Associate Professor, School of Education, Hebrew University, Jerusalem.

DAVID GORDIS
> Vice-President and Assistant Professor in Talmud, University of Judaism, Los Angeles.

ELI GRAD
> President and Dean of Faculty, Hebrew College, Boston.

MOSHE GREENBERG
> Professor of Bible, Hebrew University, Jerusalem.

ROBERT A. HAMMER
> Rabbi, Beth Hillel Congregation, Wilmette, Illinois.

YEHIEL HAYON
> Chairman, Division of Hebrew Language and Literature, The Ohio State University.

Conferees

AVRAHAM HOLTZ
Professor of Modern Hebrew Literature and Dean of Academic Development, The Jewish Theological Seminary of America.

WILLIAM B. LAKRITZ
Director of Educational Priorities, Gratz College, Philadelphia.

SID Z. LEIMAN
Associate Professor of Religious Studies, Yale University.

DAVID LIEBER
President and Samuel A. Fryer Professor in Bible, University of Judaism, Los Angeles; Vice Chancellor, The Jewish Theological Seminary of America.

YAAKOV MASHIAH
Assistant Professor of Hebrew Language and Literature, The Ohio State University.

FLORENCE MELTON
Philanthropist, industrialist.

SAMUEL M. MELTON
Founder, The Melton Research Center for Jewish Education; philanthropist, industrialist.

ELAINE I. MORRIS
Education Co-ordinator, The Melton Research Center.

LOUIS NEWMAN
Executive Director, Bureau of Jewish Education of Greater Boston.

ELAD PELED
Director General, Ministry of Education, Israel.

MARC LEE RAPHAEL
Associate Professor of History, The Ohio State University.

ARYEH ROHN
Educational Director, East Midwood Jewish Center; President, Educators Assembly.

GERALDINE ROSENFIELD
>Research analyst, American Jewish Committee.

NAHUM SARNA
>Golding Professor of Biblical Studies, Brandeis University.

ALEXANDER SCHINDLER
>President, Union of American Hebrew Congregations.

ISMAR SCHORSCH
>Rabbi Herman Abramowitz Associate Professor in Jewish History and Director of Doctoral Programs for the Institute for Advanced Studies in the Humanities, The Jewish Theological Seminary of America.

JOSEPH J. SCHWAB
>William Rainey Harper Professor Emeritus of Biological Sciences and Professor of Education, University of Chicago; Visiting Fellow, Center for the Study of Democratic Institutions.

DAVID SIDORSKY
>Professor of Philosophy, Columbia University.

RALPH W. TYLER
>Director Emeritus, Center for Advanced Study in the Behavioral Sciences.

SAUL P. WACHS
>Assistant Professor and Director of Jewish Education, Graduate Center for Contemporary Jewish Studies, Brandeis University; Visiting Professor of Jewish Education, The Jewish Theological Seminary of America.

NATHAN H. WINTER
>Professor of Education and Chairman, Department of Hebrew Culture and Education, New York University.

DAVID ZISENWINE
>Rabbi, Tifereth Israel Congregation, Columbus, Ohio.

PREFACE

The chief problem facing the Jewish community is often reduced to such shibboleths as Jewish survival, Jewish identity or Jewish education. Other diagnosticians focus on the supposed breakdown of Jewish family life or on the attrition in the centrality of the synagogue in Jewish community life.

I submit that these diagnoses are not only simplistic, but are actually wide of the mark. The conference reported in this volume gives testimony that Jewish education, for all its shortcomings, has adapted remarkably well to the special needs of Jewish communities in an open society. In the short span of four generations, American Jews, most of whom arrived here as penniless immigrants, have established several systems of education which would do credit to a more affluent community with a far longer history. Aware that the Jewish experience in America was and would continue to be different from any that preceded it, they set about immediately creating several major institutions. Among them was The Jewish Theological Seminary of America, one of the guiding forces of American Jewish life. This institution was charged with the achievement of three tasks: it was to train rabbis for American pulpits; it was to establish a center of native Jewish scholarship; and perhaps most important, it was to create channels leading from this collegium of scholars to every home, school, synagogue, and other organization of the Jewish community, and back again, so that scholars might be constantly alert to the needs of the communities for which they were translating and reinterpreting the tradition.

During the 89 years of its history, the Seminary has been striving to fulfill these expectations. Its graduates today serve some 800 congregations, countless schools, boards of Jewish education and other communal enterprises. They are skilled and knowledgeable mediators of an honored heritage for new communal needs. They understand and teach that relevance inheres in the tradition, to be demonstrated anew in each generation through authentic scholarship and creative interpretation.

As a center of Jewish scholarship, the Seminary has attained worldwide recognition. It has attracted scholars of eminence in all areas of Judaica; it has been privileged to train such scholars. It has assembled a library and museum which serve as magnets to attract those who understand the importance of these incomparable resources of research. It has become a scholarly community which offers the inestimable values of collegiality and peer criticism to students and scholars who might otherwise find themselves isolated in their field of specialization on other campuses.

The most difficult, as well as the most important, of the three goals is that of establishing channels of communication between scholar and community. For it is this network alone which can at once define and solve the basic problem of the American Jewish community. The open society requires the creation of special vehicles of communication for which a closed social system has no need. The establishment of a continuum from academic center to synagogue to home to school must be a conscious goal in America, for no one of these institutions, no matter how excellent, can function effectively, or even exist, in a vacuum.

My distinguished teacher and predecessor, Dr. Louis Finkelstein, strove to focus the energies of the scholars on the needs of the burgeoning Jewish community in America, and to interpret the conclusions of Seminary scholars for the thousands of American Jews, at every educational level, who were seeking new formulations for questions about the nature of Judaism, and new answers to old questions.

In 1963, he encouraged Professor Seymour Fox, then Dean of the Seminary's Teachers Institute, to assemble a group of Seminary faculty members, and ask them to identify those values in Jewish traditional sources which are crucial to the development of character, and to the translation of Jewish tradition as a living force in modern life. Part of the task was to establish norms based upon tradition, but also bearing the seeds of disciplined and legitimate change necessary in an evolving world.

Recognizing that American Jewish scholarship had achieved excellence and authenticity, Dr. Finkelstein and his associates understood that its next task was to mediate and radiate its achievements so that they would reach into every Jewish home. The Seminary was fortunate at this juncture in finding Mr. Samuel Mendel Melton, a man who shared both the ideal and a vision of how that ideal could be translated into reality. The result, under the inspired leadership of Dr. Fox, was the Melton Research Center for Jewish Education. That center serves today as the research arm of the Seminary's total education program, the instrument which enlists the efforts of scholars to interpret the tradition, and works with educators and others to mediate their interpretations and translate their research into school curricula at various levels. Through the Melton Research Center for Jewish Education, the bridge between these two groups has grown wider and stronger, and Judaica scholars involved in its operations have become sensitive to the needs of the Jewish schools, and increasingly willing to assume responsibility for their curricula. Uppermost in the Center's concern has been the effort to achieve a modern Jewish *paideia,* which would once again make of Torah the pervasive force that it has always been in great periods of Jewish creativity. Such a *paideia* would include not only knowledge of classical texts in the original language, but a total ethos that would reflect a Jewish response to modernity and a Jewish articulation of genuine modernity.

While progress has been made, our goal remains not adequacy, but excellence. The conference on which this book is based, sponsored jointly by the Seminary Melton Research Center for Jewish Education and the Jewish Studies Program of Ohio State University, was a significant step in refining methods to approaching that goal. Its emphasis on Jewish *paideia* was the first in the attempt to create an important synthesis in Jewish scholarship — a continuum from the scholar who confronts the source material, through the educator translating the creative results of scholarship into curriculum, to the student — from six to sixty — seeking within Judaism for the values which will make life more meaningful and more rewarding. Hopefully this volume will serve to disseminate the concerns of the Seminary and its Melton Center to an ever wider audience.

This enterprise will not create a perfect society or a scintillating system of Jewish education. It can, however, if continued with the same energies, the same flexibility and freshness of vision which marks this volume and the conference which inspired it, help us to define our problems in all their complexity and to focus on genuine diagnoses and solutions. Continuing cooperation among scholars, between scholars and educators, and between educators and pupils will insure an orderly progress toward our shared goals. Hopefully we shall achieve a new American Jewish *paideia,* and our Seminary will reflect the coming of age of our Jewish community, at the same time that it continues to inspire and lead that community

Preface

to new and higher levels of achievement, as well as constant
enrichment and revision of the structure and content of Jewish
culture and life.

New York, 1976   Gerson D. Cohen

ACKNOWLEDGMENT

In the preface, Chancellor Gerson D. Cohen speaks of the inspiration and encouragement provided by Dr. Louis Finkelstein, Seminary Chancellor when the Melton Research Center was founded, and of the remarkable vision of Samuel Mendel Melton, who made possible the founding. The conference on scholarship and curriculum and this volume are but two manifestations of their major contributions to the enhancement of Jewish education in the United States.

On assuming the Chancellorship, Professor Cohen continued to encourage and energize the work of the Center. The success of the conference was due in no small part to his leadership.

Professor Joseph J. Schwab has been consultant to the Center from its inception and his influential role is discerned in the many Melton materials issued. He is, furthermore, regarded as their mentor by the Center staff, faculty members, and students who have come under his tutelage. Professor Ralph Tyler, a member of the Academic Board and advisor on numerous projects, has generously shared his learning and experience with us.

Louis Newman, director of the Center for over a dozen years, was initiator and guide for the many teacher-training programs conducted and materials prepared. His concern with quality and standards has raised the professional levels of teachers and schools in a considerable number of Jewish communities.

As Associate Dean of the undergraduate colleges of the Seminary, Sylvia Ettenberg helped plan and supervise many of the Center's programs. Her experience and sensitivity to Jewish

Acknowledgement

educational needs are a significant factor in the Center's productivity. In this work, and particularly for the Ohio State conference, she has been effectively assisted by Dr. Elaine Morris, now director of the Center.

Those who participated in the conference discussions and the administration of the Ohio State University, which generously provided the facilities, contributed in their ways to a most successful first hearing of the papers now comprising this book.

To all we acknowledge our gratitude.

The Editors

INTRODUCTION

The Melton Research Center was established as a department of the Jewish Theological Seminary of America in 1960 by a grant from Samuel Mendel Melton of Columbus, Ohio to investigate ways and means for improving Jewish education in the United States.

Among the first projects undertaken by the Center were the preparation and testing of new materials for teaching the Bible and Jewish history. The materials were experimented with in a variety of classroom situations and were closely observed by the Melton Faculty Seminar, a committee of scholars in Judaica, the social sciences, and education. The Seminar members engaged in numerous and lengthy discussions with rabbis, teachers, parents, and students to arrive at a better understanding of the effect of the Melton program. In all such sessions it was repeatedly emphasized that the critical problem facing Jewish education was the intellectually impoverished state of existing Jewish schools.

The Faculty Seminar concluded that a proper Jewish education would help develop human beings whose lives as individuals and community members are guided by the insights of the Jewish tradition. Such an education requires not only mastery of the great Jewish texts, but the transformation of the texts' essential philosophy into life forces.

It is an educational approach which calls for the merging of many and diverse talents. Jewish scholars must locate the values in traditional sources that are to be internalized by the young. Behavioral scientists must help develop the means by which these values can best be transmitted and internalized. Teachers and educational administrators must create the tech-

niques which test both theory and practice as they are introduced into the classroom.

Fifteen years of experience provided evidence that a crucial need of the Jewish school is a curriculum based upon the
central themes of traditional Jewish thought.* The Bible, rabbinic Judaism, past and contemporary Jewish history, the prayer book, *mitzvot,* and even the Hebrew language, should be
studied in terms of the ideas they offer and the obligations
they impose.

The Melton administration being somewhat apprehen-
sive about introducing so unorthodox a proposal, called a conference in January 1973 to examine thoroughly and publicly
the implications of our decision. Representatives of Ortho-
dox, Reform, and Conservative Judaism — professors in the
disciplines of history, philosophy, Bible, literature, rabbin-
ics, and education, and concerned laymen — were asked to
consider carefully the direction in which the Center must move
if Jewish thought is to be at the core of the new curriculum of
the Jewish school.

The logic that would guide the conference was evident.
If we are committed to teaching ideas, ideas which must be
taught in their authentic formulations to young people, then
scholarship is critical for the school curriculum. But the technique of translating scholarship into curriculum is complex,
placing many unexpected obstacles in the way of scholars and
educators.

Professor Joseph Schwab, for years chairman of the Melton Academic Board and one of the architects of the Melton
program, had made a major contribution to the scholar-curric-

---

* For a more thorough discussion of this problem, see my article "Toward
a General Theory of Jewish Education" in *The Future of the Jewish Community in America* (David Sidorsky, ed.), New York: Basic Books, 1973.

Introduction

ulum problem in general education, and had worked in this area with the Melton Faculty Seminar. We asked him, therefore, to open the conference with a discussion of the many problems related to the application of the fruits of scholarship and research to elementary and secondary curricula.

Since it was important to observe how problems of translation from scholarship to curriculum manifest themselves in specific disciplines, we planned two case studies for conference consideration. Professor Gerson Cohen, Chancellor of the Seminary, eminent historian, and leading member of the Melton Faculty Seminar, was invited to present one study, and we believe it brings a novel intellectual dimension to the teaching of history. As our second discipline we chose Jewish traditional thought, and were fortunately able to call upon Professor Marvin Fox, outstanding teacher of philosophy, who demonstrated that the significance of Jewish ideas for the curriculum goes beyond the boundaries of any specific set of Jewish commitments.

Our fourth session was devoted to the needs of the community. Rabbi Alexander Schindler, president of the Union of American Hebrew Congregations, was the distinguished proponent of the community's needs and demands. His insights into the tensions between scholars and representatives of the community were illuminating, and he delivered an eloquent plea for a Jewish education program designed to alleviate such tensions.

Professor Ralph Tyler, dean of educational academia, and the most influential figure in curriculum study in the United States, has been a participant in the Melton program from the outset. He very kindly agreed to lead the closing session, helping us take the decisive step toward curricular implementation.

My paper, revised following the conference, attempts to emphasize the complexity of the progression from plan to practice, particularly as brought to light during the conference sessions.

Each paper presented was followed by lengthy discussion. I regret it was not possible to include the discussions in this volume for they were lively, erudite cross-examinations, sparked with acute observations. A glance at the list of forty participants will show them to be academic and community leaders from important centers of learning in the United States and Israel. Their criticisms and recommendations were heeded and are reflected in the proposal for a Jewish school curriculum rooted in the basic ideas of the Jewish tradition which we are now developing for the Melton Research Center.

Jerusalem 1976   Seymour Fox

1

TRANSLATING SCHOLARSHIP INTO CURRICULUM[1]

Joseph J. Schwab

Agents of Translation

The means by which scholarly materials are adapted to the purposes of education are quickly told but only slowly mastered. The means are easily understood but difficult to use. They are difficult because they require collaboration by men of five different bodies of experience, each such body of experience often being alien to the possessors of the other bodies of experience. The collaborators, then, must first learn something of the concerns, values and operations which arise from each other's experience. They must then, and this is harder, learn slowly to honor these various groupings of concerns, values, operations, and adapt and diminish each his own values to make room in his thinking for the others. Finally, they must bring these partially coalesced bodies of judgmental factors to bear on the body of scholarly materials.

These three operations — discovery of one another by the collaborators, coalescence of what is discovered, utilization of the coalesced body of concerns as tools for generating new educational materials and purposes — take place, not serially, but simultaneously. The first two take place as the third is undertaken and carried forward in a spiral movement toward a body of generated educational alternatives, and choices among them,

1

choices which satisfy entirely no one party to the collaboration but which do satisfy the collective more than does any other constellation of educational means and purposes among those considered.

What are the five bodies of experience which ought to be represented in the group which undertakes the task of curriculum revision? (In what follows, the words, "first," "second," and so on are not to be taken as indicating logical or operational status, but only as convenient enumerations.)

First, there must be someone familiar with the scholarly materials under treatment and with the discipline from which it comes. Supposing that the materials under consideration are historical, for example, this is to say that some one of the group must be familiar not only with this body of historical material but must also know what it is to be an historian. The reason for this dual emphasis will be clarified later.

Second, there must be someone familiar with the children who are to be the beneficiaries of the curricular operation. This experience, too, should be manifold. It should include, at one pole, on one axis, general knowledge of the age group under consideration: what it already knows, what it is ready to learn, what will come easy to it, what difficult, what aspirations and anxieties must be taken into account as facilitations and handicaps to learning, what will appear to the child as contributing to a present want or need. At the other pole of this axis, the experience should include intimate knowledge of the children under consideration, knowledge achieved by direct involvement with them. This intimate knowledge is required in order to know the ways in which this particular group of children (the middle-class Jewish children of Columbus, Ohio, for example) depart from generalities about middle-class children of a given age. Such known special attributes will include not only some impression of the direction and degree to which these children depart from the average on the scales used by the gatherers of general knowledge but also will include knowledge of attitudes, competences, propensities, not taken into account by the gatherers of general knowledge about children.

Experience of children should also include a range of knowledge concerning their present state of mind and heart treated as a stage toward the children's probable fate: who and what they are likely to become as adults. This would include, for example, some of the probabilities about their future economic status and function; what leisure they will enjoy; what adult aspirations and attitudes are likely to characterize them, their friends and neighbors; what roles they will play in the political community, the ethnic or religious community, the family.

These references to community suggest the third body of experience which should be represented in the curriculum-making group: experience of the milieus in which the child's learning will take place and its fruits be brought to bear. The relevant milieus are, again, manifold, nesting one in another like Chinese boxes. Moving from the smaller toward the larger, the milieus include, first, the school and the schoolroom in which the learning and teaching is supposed to occur. What is likely to be children's relations to one another? Will the classroom group largely overlap the play or neigborhood group, or other group in which the children function; e.g., will the children begin as friends and acquaintances or as relative strangers? Will their relationship be dominated by cliques or other subgroups? What structure of authority (or status) will characterize the relations of teachers of the school to one another and to the educational leaders of the school? In what ways are these relations of adults in the school likely to affect the relations of teachers to students or to what and how the teachers are likely to teach?

The relevant milieus will also include the congregational community, the particular grouping of the religious, class, or ethnic genus. What aspirations, styles of life, attitudes toward education, ethical standards (or lack of ethical standards), for example, characterize these parents and, through their roles as parents, affect the children as well as affect the character of what can and cannot be attempted?

These two examples of relevant milieus suggest the remainder. What are the relations of this congregation to other congregations of the same religious, ethnic, or class genus; what similarities or differences of rite or habit characterize them? And what they do or do not do? What are the relations of the entire religious, ethnic, or class genus to the other genera which constitute the town or city and are represented in miniature by the children of each genus as they interact with children of other genera in the playground and public school? What is the condition, dominant preoccupation, and cultural climate of the whole policy and its social classes, insofar as these may affect the careers, the probable fate, and the ego identity of the children whom we are teaching? (A dominant anti-intellectualism, for example, a focus on material acquisition, a high value on conformity to a nationwide pattern and on cloaking of cultural-religious differences.)

So far, then, three bodies of experience to be represented in the curriculum group: experience of the subject matter and its discipline; of the child; of the communities or milieus. The fourth required body of experience is experience of the teachers. This experience should clearly include probable knowledge of what these teachers know and how flexible and ready they are likely to be in learning new materials and new ways of teaching. We need good guesses, too, about the personalities, characters, and prevailing moods of the teachers: how they are likely to relate to the children, to one another, to the directors of the school, to visiting master teachers or scholars; how they tend to feel about and in themselves. It may well be desirable to know something of the backgrounds of these teachers: what biases they bring with them as part of their own secular or religious education, what political affiliations they strongly feel.

The fifth required body of experience is with the curriculum-making process itself. We have remarked on the need for each representative of a body of experience to discover the experience of the others and the relevance of these radically different experiences to curriculum making; of the need for a partial coalescence of these bodies of experience. These are necessary, "concurrent preliminaries" to the actual process of making a defensible curriculum which has some likelihood of functioning effectively. They are necessary preliminaries which are highly unlikely to occur of themselves. The common developing behavior of such curriculum groups operating without a representative of this fifth body of experience is one of resentful or resigned submission of three of the group to a fourth. It is very easy for the scholar-specialist to overawe the group and to impose the character and structure of his discipline as the correct model for the character and structure of the curriculum. Only if the representative with knowledge of and sympathy with the children intervenes as an equal in the deliberation is the discipline represented by the scholar likely to be treated as a resource of education rather than as a model for it.

It is often easy for the representative of the children to overwhelm the scholar with his warnings of what children will and will not do, can and cannot do, thus opposing his sources of expertise — what children have habitually done in older curricula taught by their own appropriate methods — to the efforts of the scholar to urge trial of new purposes sought by new means. It is similarly possible for the representative of the milieus successfully to urge the conventional caution that a mere member or part of a complex structure cannot hope to change the whole of which he is a mere part, or effect even a partial change contrary to prevailing habits and attitudes. Similarly, it is possible for him who knows the teaching group to urge conformity of the curriculum to what teachers currently can do and are willing to do.

One task of the representative of the curriculum-making process is to function as a countervailing force to these common tendencies. It is he who, at the start, reminds all others present of the importance of the experience of each to the curriculum-making enterprise. It is he, in the role of chairman, who monitors the proceedings, pointing out to the group what has happened in the course of their deliberations, what is currently taking place, what has not been considered which ought to be considered, what subordinations and superordinations of considerations may have occurred to the detriment or facilitation of the processes all are engaged upon.

Where the first function of the curriculum specialist concerns the concurrent preliminaries to the curriculum-making process, the second concerns curriculum-making itself. It is the curriculum specialist who knows the concrete embodiments, the material objects, which are the indispensable constituents of a curriculum. For it is a mistake to suppose that a curriculum planning group can safely and appropriately terminate its activities merely with statements of purposes and explanation of the reasons for choice of these rather than other purposes.

It cannot so terminate its activities because curricular purposes and reasons for them must be communicated by language, by formulation. Such formulations, for reasons too large to be treated well now, will inevitably fall short of encompassing the full meanings and real intentions of the parties to the curricular deliberation. The meanings which matter are those which determine whether a given text, a given pattern of teaching, a given treatment of a topic, when examined and momentarily submitted to, is both felt and seen to be appropriate to the curriculum which has been envisaged. These meanings lie in the whole course of the deliberations which created them. The meanings lie as much in what was decided against, for example, as in what was decided for. They lie in the reasons for rejection of alternatives as much as in the reasons for preferring those which are preferred. They lie in nuances of expression in the course of the deliberation.

These are meanings which are difficult or impossible to encompass in a formulation to be read and acted upon by individuals who were not privy to the deliberation and become related to the deliberation only by a terminal formulation of its chosen purposes and reasons. Consequently, it is unrealistic, in a highly charged and special meaning of "unrealistic," to expect that others, not privy to the deliberation, can, like bronze molders, take a terminal statement of purposes as a pattern and, from it, realize a curriculum, i.e., construct materials for students, guides for teachers, patterns of teaching and learning which are the appropriate materials, guides, and patterns.

Equally, however, a curriculum planning group can rarely afford either the time or the expertise necessary for the construction of embodiments of the curriculum. Others must be enlisted in the effort in collaboration with the planning group, a collaboration which proceeds by formulation followed by discussion of what the reader of the formulation has garnered from it, followed by trial construction of a bit of concrete curriculum, followed by scrutiny of this essay by the planning group, followed by discussion of it among both makers of the bit and planners, followed by a corrected bit or an additional bit, and so on.

The second function of the curriculum specialist is to instigate, administer, and chair this process of realization of the curriculum.

There is a second way in which terminal formulation fails to encompass and communicate the real intentions of a planning group. This second inadequacy stems from the deep psychology of intentions *per se*. Espoused educational intentions are specified and projected values of the planning group, values possessed and understood in terms much broader than education, and very much broader than any one concrete bit of educational curriculum. The breadth and generality of these values are so great, indeed, that only in the rare instance can a merely rationally guided, concrete specification of a stated educational intention be confidently identified by merely rational means as embodying or satisfying one or more of the broad values held by the planning group. Only if there be added to rational scrutiny of a proposed segment of a curriculum a felt experience of it, an undergoing — at least in imagination and empathy — can it be identified with some confidence as probably appropriate.

This statement about values and intentions can be summarized by saying that what we usually distinguish as ends and means — stated curricular intentions and curricular materrials — are more realistically to be seen as elements in a maturation process by which values are realized reflexively. A value is embodied in a stated educational intention but only equivocally and very imperfectly. The stated intention then serves as a highly imperfect guide or pattern for construction of a curriculum bit. Experience of the curriculum bit reduces by a little the equivocation of the stated intention and illuminates a little more the value which lies at its roots. Substitution of another curriculum bit, or modification of the bit, may ensue on the illuminating experience but there will also be reflexive modification of the formulated intention itself or modification of the way it is understood. Or there may be discard or replacement of it. The underlying value which gave rise to the stated intention has itself come closer to the surface and may be better understood. The value may even be so well illuminated that it becomes accessible to scrutiny, criticism, and change. At least we may hope that, though the value may not be examined with an eye to changing it as a living value of the curriculum planner, it is scrutinized with an eye to whether it should be imposed upon the student, the child, by way of the curriculum.

Instigation, encouragement, and monitoring of this process is a third function of the curriculum specialist.

There are, then, five bodies of experience which must be brought together to effect valid translation of scholarly materials into defensible curricular materials. It does not follow that five persons are required. The group may be smaller or larger than five. It may be smaller to the extent that two or more of the required bodies of experience can be found in one person. The member who knows the child may also know the milieus, for example, or the teachers. The scholar may himself have adequate and still living experience of the child or of teachers.

There are also reasons why the group should be larger than five. Our knowledge of social milieus and of the development of children is knowledge produced out of the variform disciplines of the behavioral sciences. Different investigators in such sciences go about their enquiries in different ways, guided by differing conceptions of problem, method, and principle of investigation. Consequently, more than one useful body of knowledge arises about an approximately common subject matter. Too often the purveying possessor of such knowledge possesses only one of the several useful bodies of knowledge about the subject matter in question and needs very much to be complemented and corrected by another purveying specialist who knows another of the relevant bodies of knowledge.

The same pluralism holds for scholarly disciplines. There are dozens of critical conceptions of the novel and short story. There are manifold conceptions of the character of historical investigation and knowledge, of moral-political behavior, of the ways in which appropriate religious behavior should be determined. Some measure of these pluralisms should be represented in the curriculum-making group if there is not to be embodiment of doctrine so narrow as to invite rejection when it sees the light of day.

Even experience of the curriculum might well be supplied in more than one person. For one such person will be possessor of values of his own as well as possessor of curricular expertise. Consequently, only one such person in the role of chairman might well suppress some aspects of the deliberation rather than evoke them. If the notion of two chairmen is too bizarre to be acceptable, then let us say, at least, that some additional person should be present to monitor the behavior of the chairman, someone alert to the movement of discussion, alert to its purport and removed from both the discipline under translation and from the educational purposes it is intended to serve. I am not clear as to how this monitoring function is to be served and leave to others, better equipped, the task of coping with this problem.

Material to be Translated

All the foregoing is grounded in the fact that defensible educational thought must take account of four commonplaces or topics which are of equal rank: the learner, the teacher, the milieu, and the subject matter. None of these can be omitted without omitting a vital factor in educational thought and practice. No one of them may be allowed to dominate the deliberation unless that domination is itself conscious and capable of defense in terms of the circumstances of the deliberation. This is to say, of course, that despite the many educational bandwagons which bear witness to the contrary, neither the child nor the society, nor subject matters, nor teachers, are properly the centers of curriculum. (Indeed, the origin of bandwagons — curriculums which have a merry but short life — often arise from just such an overemphasis: the child-centered curriculums of Progressivism; the social-change centered curriculums of the nineteen thirties; the subject-matter curriculums coming out of recent curriculum reforms; the teacher-centered curriculums which may arise from unionism in education.)

That coordination and not superordination-subordination is the proper relation of these commonplaces can be seen by considering the possible dominion of one in the light of another. Let us take subject matter and student as our representative cases. Imagine, then, a child-centered planning which emphasizes above all else, the present inclinations of students, the interest they bring with them or those which can be roused by the shrewd placement of provocative objects and events in the educational space. In a curriculum so initiated and thoughtfully planned, the other three commonplaces will not be ignored. Indeed, they may be honored, but in a subordinate role. The milieus will be honored as limiting conditions by being examined with an eye to predicting interests and facilitating planning of curricular activities. The milieus will be honored as targets of education by emphases in which collaboration of children, establishment of "rules of the game," and the role of umpire made necessary by rules, constitute socializing aspects of

the curriculum. Subject matters will be honored by being constituted the source from which and by which selection is made of
the provocative objects and events which serve as catalysts of
curricular activity. The teacher will be honored as the person
who will most often serve in the role of umpire and serve more
extensively as the maturer member of the learning community.

Despite these honorings of the other three commonplaces of
education, the dominance of the fourth, the child, creates clear
and present ground for worry with respect to the subject-matter
factors. The core of the worry comes through as the question,
"But what of the many things the children may *not* learn which
they need to know?" We hear this core concern reverberate in
the question whether any planner, any teacher, can know
enough, can know variety enough and choose wisely enough
among so many bodies of knowledge to plant in the learning area
the appropriate provocatives of interest and learning. We hear
the concern echo again in the question, "But what if the 'provocative' objects do not provoke?" And these worries are
properly not allayed by the assurance that a knowledge which is
truly needed in the days when the child is no longer a child will
be sought and learned. For we know of nothing and are given
nothing in the way of evidence to support this reassurance.

In such worries we are tacitly affirming, and correctly
affirming, that subject matters — bodies of knowledge, of
competencies, of attitudes, propensities, and values — constitute
the most inclusive and most telling check list of possible de-
sirables and possible human interests which mankind possesses.
It is this characteristic of subject matter which makes it one of the
coordinate commonplaces of education.

This characteristic of subject matter appears to argue also
for subject matter as the ruling commonplace of curricular deliberation. But recall what occurs and is likely to occur again

when subject-matter concerns initiate the planning of curriculum. In the first place, most subject matters are bodies of knowledge. As knowledge, they tend to shut out from view those other bodies of educables: competences, attitudes, propensities, values. As bodies of knowledge, they are organized. There is a thread which leads us from one bit of the subject matter to the next. Each bit appears to be contingent on what went before and to make necessary what comes after. It becomes gravely difficult, then, to select within the subject matter for those parts of it which are made defensible in the curriculum because they serve the child, the teaching function, or the polity. Above all, in a curriculum enterprise which begins in an effort to adapt a given subject matter to curricular purposes, it is virtually impossible to question whether that subject matter as a whole is desirable in the curriculum (against criteria emerging from the other commonplaces), whether it should be given much or little time and energy inevitably taken from other subject matters or other curricular activities.

Again, there is clear and present ground for worry, this time with respect to the child as a factor. Is this subject matter worthy, now or in the future, of the time and energy demanded of the child? Has there been generous and just concern to apportion time to it, relative to time apportioned to other subject matters, with respect to what is better and worse for children — or has the decision been made by the weightiness, the dignity, the current esteem in which the subject matter is held? Or because the curriculum planners are constituted of (or dominated by) lovers of that subject matter? We hear this core concern reverberate in the question whether every subject matter is equally accessible to all children, or equally useful to all children, or whether individual differences, regional differences, many other grouping differences among children, ought not determine how much of a given subject matter should be taught, what different selections ought to be made for different children, and what different versions and emphases, even in a single selection of content, ought to be made in the interest of the needs and abilities of different children. The reverberation is heard again as we wonder but what the heavy hand of self-interested adulthood may be bearing too heavily on childhood and whether the past, and what the past found useful, may be weighing heavily on the present and the future.

Through such worries we are affirming that in a consideration of a subject matter as affording materials for curriculum, the ultimate criterion must be what is best, or good, or satisfying to the learner as a child, as a human being, and as a citizen.

Our worries in these two cases taken together affirm that the commonplaces ought to be coordinate in the planning of curriculum. Amid the concerns of the child-centered planning, we note the vital role of organized subject matter. Amid concerns for subject matter, we note the vital role of the child's present and future.

All this, however, fails to speak directly to the practical problem of how to maintain coordinacy. For the practical problem arises from the fact that a group of men is rarely commissioned or financed to think about *education*. (If they were, half of the practical problem would disappear, since the very question raises all the commonplaces to equal visibility.) Instead, men are usually commissioned and financed to think about satisfying manpower requirements of the state or how to "modernize" the curriculum in biology, in social studies, in physics, in English literature. And such questions immediately raise the flag of one commonplace above the others.

Four factors, no one sufficient in itself, no one indispensable, seem to me to speak to this problem. The first factor is the make-up of the planning group. In the ordinary course of events, the nucleus of a group commissioned to translate a body of scholarly material into curriculum is drawn from the discipline or dsciplines to be dealt with. It is the members of this nucleus who make the curricular decisions. Men who represent the child, the teacher, and the milieu are usually drawn in only as subordinate, temporary "consultants" who speak their inadequate piece and depart. Their piece is inadequate. They can speak only in generalities. They cannot speak to problems of the subject matter because they have not been peers in the discussion of it. They cannot speak to concrete curricular alternatives because they have not been witnesses or parties to the generation of them from the scholarly body of material. The design of the deliberating body virtually guarantees, indeed, that commonplaces other than that of the subject matter be effectively silent.

Part of the solution to this problem is obvious: inclusion as peers in the deliberating group from the start of representatives of all four commonplaces. Almost as obvious is the need that these representatives of the other commonplaces be men who are not overawed by the scholar. But let us go a step farther. Let us require that the first order of business be explanation of the scholarly material by the representative of that material to the skeptical ears and minds of the remainder of the group. Let these unawed skeptics question the specialist closely and pointedly, indeed, personally, on all matters that are unclear, on all un-supported assertions about the importance or the character of his field and of the particular body of materials which is to be treated. Let there be questions about adequacy of problem and of evidence in the scholarship which produced the material. Let there be questions about the existence of competing questions and competing solutions. In brief, let us establish from the beginning the place of the scholarly member as only one among many and not the place of "first among peers."

The second desirable factor toward solution of the practical problem of maintaining coordinacy of the commonplace is a process of evaluation of tentatively accepted bits of curriculum, which operates concurrently with the deliberations (not after "formative" evaluation). The notion of formative evaluation refers to when the evaluation is to occur and to the use to which it is to be put. It is to be done in course; it is to be done in order to improve curricular materials before they are distributed for wide use. We are concerned, however, with a notion of "improvement" which goes considerably beyond the usual. The usual concern is for the efficiency with which the curricular bit serves the stated intention which generated it. We are concerned, in addition, with clarification of the intention itself and of the values from which it arises. Consequently, the character of the evaluation as well as its timing and use require specification.

It should be an evaluation which goes distinctly beyond test of efficiency. It should aim toward methods which will break the limits imposed by the stated intention. I have in mind an evaluation procedure in which the evaluator joins the experimental teachers in the actual classroom situation in which the materials are tested. The two of them, teacher and evaluator, are to engage in an alert, sensitive, scanning watch to identify any and all reactions and responses of children as they deal with the materials under treatment with a special eye for reactions and responses unanticipated in the stated intention. From the identified reactions and responses unanticipated in the stated intention, evaluator and teacher select those which they deem most representative of unanticipated characteristics of the curriculum bit and which seem to them most significant to the education and development of the child. (This selection may be done, and should be done, with the curriculum specialist member of the

planning group.) The frequency and intensity of these selected
untoward reactions are then measured. Most important of all, the
selected reactions are to be disclosed to the planning group in
two embodiments — not only in the usual formulated statement
of the evaluator, his statistical report, but by arranging with the
teacher for direct confrontation of members of the planning
group with the student behaviors themselves. This is to say that
teacher and evaluator stage demonstration classes (and class
aftermaths) for the deliberating body. This is the confrontation
through which, hopefully, the planners will be able to go beyond
rational scrutiny of what they are doing toward a felt experience,
an undergoing, of what they are proposing to do to and with the
children. (This is one way in which the child, as one important
commonplace of curriculum consideration, can speak for himself.)

  Let us turn now to consideration of two important attitudes
which should be taken toward scholarly materials when they are
translated into curriculum. First, they must be treated as resources for curriculum — a matter mentioned earlier but not
developed. The import of this notion of "resource" is best con-
veyed by an instance of its contrary and an instance of its affirmation. The field of literature will serve as a source of
instances.

  I have before me a statement which introduces a slim
volume called *Discussion of the Short Story*.[2] It reads:

  A short story is neither plot nor character nor statement
  nor style; it is simultaneously plot and character and
  statement and style. In language a short story records
  moving character reflecting an attitude toward existence.
  The elements of the experience are separable only for
  the pleasures of discussion. For authoritative com-

munication with any story, we return to the complicated
experience of the story itself.

If I interpret this passage correctly, the author is (a) asserting a
definition of the character of the "scholarly" material under
treatment, a definitive definition, if you will permit me, one
which asserts precisely and completely the character of the
material. He is (b) asserting that translation of short stories into
curriculum must, by whatever means will work, treat the short
story as what it is: the curriculum must realize the short story in
the minds, hearts, and palates of the student in its full character,
or, at any rate, try to do so as far as the condition of the students
permits.

The passage as interpreted is thus a sterling instance of
refusal to use scholarly material as a curriculum resource. It
insists on conformity of the curriculum to the nature of its source
materials. The dominion of subject matter is made virtually
complete; the other commonplaces are virtually ignored; the
student, the child, is treated as indefinitely malleable clay to be
given the shape dictated by the material.

Compare that passage as interpreted with another, taken
from a paper titled *Literature in the Revitalized Curriculum.* [3]

In more recent time... the new English [has been] rather
much under the supervision of the academic.... We are
now, in my view, on the threshold of the fourth stage,
which I shall call the Humanitarian. If there is a "new
English"... it has taken the development of the imagination, conceived in the most liberating sense, as its
ultimate aim.... The imagination is no narrow faculty,
but filters through and colors every part, every corner
of our lives. Let us take for example the matter of
morality.... The curriculum should be open to a great

> variety of values and visions, including those that rub
> against the grain of society... . As the teacher is con-
> cerned with developing and expanding the student's
> total imaginative capacity, so he must be concerned
> with all aspects of the imagination... .

If I interpret this passage correctly, its author, too, has started
from a characteristic of the scholarly material under consideration. But, unlike the first, he has moved immediately to concern himself with what service this characteristic can perform
which is good and satisfying for students. By this move, he
illustrates nicely what is meant by the treatment of scholarly
material as a curricular resource: the curriculum is not to con-
form to the material; the material is to be used in the service
of the student. (Incidentally, it is a nice and comforting irony
that the author of this passage, James Miller, is an academic,
a professor of English literature.)

Needless to say, the act of using scholarly materials as
resources of curriculum can be perverted and its perversion is
as pernicious educationally as its privation. Perversion consists
of warping the scholarly materials entirely out of their character
in order to force them to serve a curricular purpose which fasci-
nates the planners. Such perversions are exemplified by terminal
formulations which begin, "How can we use science (or
literature, or history, or moral dilemmas) to achieve x, or y, or
z?" And the x, y, or z, originate the deliberation and the named
scholarly materials are dragged in by the heels. In brief, the
perversion consists of degrading the subject matter as a
commonplace of education to the role of servant.

The second stance to be taken toward scholarly material
when it is translated into curriculum consists of maintaining
as frontlets before our eyes, the realization that, as scholarly

material, as well as in its role as curricular resource, it possesses three faces, is three different things. It is, first, that which it conveys. A piece of historical material is an account of what happened to someone somewhere. That event as it happened to those people at that time is one of its faces. A short story conveys a moral dilemma or a vision of a social class or the operation of a facet of human character. Any one of these constitutes one of its faces. A body of scientific material tells us something about a grouping of phenomena. That is one of the faces of a piece of scientifc material.

A piece of scholarly material is also that which produced it. It is the outcome of a discipline, a coherent way of bringing a body of principles, methods, and conceptions to bear upon some inchoate mass in order to give it order or meaning or both. A short story is the outcome of a discipline which selects material, clothes it in a certain language, gives it a certain form, selects and uses certain devices rather than others in order to evoke a certain effect. A piece of scientific material is the outcome of a discipline which predetermines the character of some selected grouping of phenomena in order to formulate questions which it can answer by means of the techniques presently available to it.

Third, a piece of scholarly material is a compound object, a complex and organized thing which requires certain disciplines addressed to it to make it wholly accessible to the reader, viewer, hearer, learner. There are numerous questions which must be addressed to a short story before that story will reveal itself in its full dimensions to the reader. There are quite different questions which must be addressed to a piece of history or of science before one of them will reveal its full purport.

Constant awareness of the existence of these three faces of every piece of scholarly material is crucial to the translation into curriculum because each face possesses and suggests its own richness of curricular possibility. The purport may have many curricular uses — and this is the face to which most curricular efforts are addressed. But the other two faces have curricular potential as great or greater than the purport taken alone. Where the purport speaks to those curricular possibilities which are sometimes summarized under the heading "knowing that," the disciplinary faces speak to the curricular possibilities which are summarized under the heading, "knowing how."

The potential curricular values of disciplines which give access to a complex work are reasonably clear. Access to the intricate content and structure of a short story, a lyric poem, a psalm, a work of plastic art, music, is access to a highly durable and virtually inexhaustible source of deep satisfaction — for some people in some times under some circumstances. The remark by Hollis Summers, quoted earlier, says as much, and he is quite right. (My concern about his remarks arise from what he does not say, the purport of the qualifications, "for some people in some times under some circumstances.") Access to a scientific work is access to ground for critical judgment which avoids the misinformations, the extremes of belief, and the confusions which are often the outcomes of popular renderings of such materials. Access to argument, whether toward political or moral action, is access to some judgment about the better and worse commitment of our time, our energy, and our developing character. Access to historical works is access to one of the factors which determine who we think we are, what problems we think we have, and how we ought to act. In general, possession of such disciplines is possession of avenues toward freedom of thought, feeling, and action.

The potential curricular values of the scholarly disciplines — such disciplines as those of rhetoric toward produc-

tion of argument, science toward production of warranted conclusions about natural things, history toward interpretations of
the past — are less obviously of potential curricular value for
the young. Their potential becomes clearer when we note what
it might mean to convey such disciplines to them.

   We do not mean that the young in general are to be made into competent historians, investigators, artists. This is a fatuous
dream. We do not mean merely that the young are to be given
thin versions of one or another scholarly discipline to be pur-
sued as a hobby. We mean, rather, that we ought to consider as
curricular possibilities the conveyance of such knowledge about
and exemplary experience with such disciplines that the student
(1) is better prepared to master those disciplines which give
access to the finished outcomes of the scholarly disciplines;
(2) is equipped with insight into the methods and various
principles of a scholarly discipline sufficient to add a critical
component to his access-disciplines. To grasp some of the many
ways in which different historians conceive the character of
historical knowledge, to identify the facts pertinent to each
one's history, and to seek out these facts, is to grasp the kind
of history one is reading at a given moment. It is to realize the
limitations of that kind as one among a number of ways of
throwing light upon the past and interpreting the present, and
it is enhanced competence to judge the dependability of the particular history under scrutiny. At the same time, the student's
ability to read such a history is enhanced: he knows more of the
questions to be addressed to the text and is better prepared to
extract answers to these questions from the text.

   In some cases, our stricture above, against conveying
a thin version of a scholarly discipline and encouraging its
actual use, is an overstatement of the case. Simple versions of
some scholarly disciplines may be of serious use to some lay-

men. Rhetoric is one of these. Since the good of every man is bound up in the communities of which he is member, the decisions made by such communities affect him. His ability to affect consensus is clearly, then, an ability which redounds to his benefit. Casuistry, the discipline by which principles (especially moral and religious principles) are scrutinized for their relevance to a situation demanding choice and action and adapted to the case, is another which can redound to the benefit of both individual student and the moral, religious, and political communities of which he is part. Some first-hand experience of scientific disciplines vastly sharpens one's understanding of what constitutes reliable and sufficient evidence for conclusions.

The possible benefit of mastery of simple versions of some "scholarly" disciplines extends into the emotive realm as well. For example, the ability to make a lyric poem, or a moving statement of praise, of thanks, of awe, or fear, is a contribution to our ability to clarify (understand) our emotions, to control them where control is desirable, to discharge them where discharge is desirable. By such means melancholy can often be transformed into realistic grief rather than deteriorate toward pathological melancholia. A debt to the character or action of another person can be shaped into worthy gratitude rather than permitted to degenerate into debthood or thoughtless worship. Similar usefulness may exist for some persons in disciplines other than the artistic. Some mastery of historical disciplines, for example, may enable us to organize and understand our own pasts, our personal histories, and thus gain some additional hold on our abilities to think about our future and plan it.

Method of Translation

The methods by which scholarly materials are translated into defensible curriculums are not mere transformations of one kind or style of material into another. They are, rather, methods for assessing privations, perversities, errors, and misdevelopments in those who are to be recipients of the putative benefits of curriculum; then, methods for discovering in scholarly materials curricular potentials which serve the purpose envisaged in the light of detected student needs; then, assessment of the probable advantages of one against others of these curricular potentials, as means toward educational benefits.

The method begins, then, in two sources: (1) in knowledge of the young students and knowledge of predecessor students now grown and exhibiting the good and bad effect of previous curriculums; (2) in a dream or vision of the best student grown (or several different "bests"), a dream or vision deriving from the values of the planning group and, presumably, of the group upon which their efforts will be imposed. In brief, the method begins with an intertwining of two radically different strands: information as one strand; soul-searching as the other.

Their intertwining is to be emphasized. Each item of one strand is to serve as an occasion for locating an item of the other strand. Each information on the present condition of students or former students ought normally to be followed by voiced discoveries of how the planners feel about the condition in question: whether it is approved, and why; if disapproved, what alternate condition or conditions ought to replace it. These should then invite statement of differences or concurrences of view on the desirability of the replacing condition and what might be done about it. Similarly, each statement of value or desired intention ought to evoke consideration of students or milieus as they are known or thought to be, with speculations on how they arrived at that desirable or undesirable condition.

This initial stage of the deliberations serves two purposes. First, precisely because the group is commissioned to concern itself with scholarly materials, it begins by emphasis on other commonplaces, especially the student and his milieus, so as to maintain coordinacy of the commonplaces. Second, it is the prime means by which each planner begins to discover himself — his values and their projection into educational intentions — begins to discover his colleagues, and begins to discover the loci at which each must begin to modify or contract himself to accommodate his colleagues' views and arrive at a collegiality which can function effectively in pursuing the task at hand.

These are purposes which justify expenditure of considerable time. I conceive as a suggestive order of magnitude, ten or fifteen two-hour meetings apportioned over as many weeks. The time should not be allotted nor should one attempt to determine its end point by some estimate of achieved consensus. It should not be a move toward consensus, but an airing and accommodation which will continue in other guises in all stages of the deliberation. The terminus of this first phase is signalled by the appearance of distaste for its continuance, a demand, generally agreed upon, that something more concrete take its place.

It is necessary to interpolate here some comment on an embarrassing matter: there is no warrant that men gathered together for the purpose outlined will discover anything of themselves or their colleagues, or modulate their views to accommodate the views of their colleagues. Collegiality will arise only to the extent that a minimal capacity for shame and a degree of humility characterize each member of the group. For it is "normal" for men to treat their own values as if they were well-examined values, to ignore contrary or different values utilized by others, and most of all, automatically to elevate the area of their own expertise to the role of ultimate arbiter of matters under consideration. These "normalities," especially the arrogance of specialism, will wreck any attempt at responsible translation of scholarly materials into defensible curriculum. I know of no device of chairmanship or tactic of administration which can avert this danger. A measure of humility and shame is our only defense.

The second phase of the deliberation is occasioned by introduction of a piece of scholarly material whose potential for the curriculum is to be determined. This phase has, in its turn, two subphases. There must be, first, the generation of alternatives. The piece of scholarly material is scrutinized in its three existences (its purport, its originating discipline, the discipline required for access to it) for its curriculum potentials. The basis for inventiveness in this regard consists of the other commonplaces, as these have come to be envisaged in the phase of self-discovery. One figuratively turns the piece of scholarly material from side to side, viewing it in different lights. What use might it serve toward more critical loyalty to a community? What might it contribute to the child's resources for satisfying activity? What might it contribute to a moral or intellectual virtue held to be desirable by the planning group? To what convictions might it lead concerning conservation or reform of a community setting? To what maturation might it contribute?

The second subphase is entered when several pieces of scholarly material have been successfully treated in the first subphase. Now there are several potential curriculum bits competing for the time and energies of the students, for place in the curriculum. The second subphase is, then, a process of choice and decision among the competing curricular bits, the intentions they seem to realize, the values they try to embody.

In this subphase the central problem consists in discovering the considerations which ought to be brought to bear on the alternatives. As in the first subphase the resources from which to derive the appropriate considerations are the commonplaces. From the subject-matter commonplace: does the purport of the material concern an important historical event or condition, for example? Is it good history, arising from well-validated facts, interpreted in a defensible way toward insights useful to our time and circumstance? From the milieu: does is contribute toward improvement of a community? Is it likely to be acceptable to that community? If it is novel or disturbing, are there steps we can take to facilitate its acceptance? From the child: is the good it is supposed to do more urgent or more important than the goods served by competing curricular bits? Is it appropriate to the age and experience of the children under consideration? What consequences may it have on the relations of child to parent and to other significant adults? What effect may it have on the relations of children to one another? What effect may it have on the relation of the child to himself? From the teacher: is he or she prepared to teach it as it should be taught? What new learning or trainings of the teacher may be required? Can these new trainings be successfully entered upon? Will the teacher be in sympathy with the values embodied in the curricular bit? If not, are there prevailing values among teachers which can be used to help enlist them in the service of the embodied values?

Needless to say, it is impossible to forecast the precise questions which ought to be asked of the alternatives under consideration. The appropriate questions are made appropriate by the character of each particular curricular bit, by the attitudes, values, and cognitive skills of the planners, by the community for which the planning is done, by the peculiarities of the children to whom the curriculum is to be submitted. (The commonplaces are operating again.) Discovery of the "right" questions to ask depends in the last analysis on the deliberative

skill of the planners and the alertness of the chairing curriculum specialist.

The role of the curriculum specialist here is one which
derives from the most marked and peculiar characteristic of
the deliberative process: that it must compare incommensurables. That is, the task is not merely a technical one of fore-
casting consequences and costs (of the mutual undergoing of
child and curriculum bit). It is not adequately stated as merely
determining the value or good of the forecast consequences.
For "the" value is in fact a number of different values: a valued
contribution to the maturity of the child; a valued effect (perhaps
negative) on the present state of mind of the child; a valued effect
on the community, and so on. These different values are the
incommensurables, which, commensurable or not, must be
weighed against one another. And there are no weighting factors
which can be supplied to the deliberating group by which to
render this process a simple one. In the last analysis, the
weighting will arise from the collegial pooling of the values of
the group.

At this point in deliberation, the special obligation of the
curriculum-specialist chairman is to ensure that the group hunt
out, recognize, and juxtapose the many different considerations
which are pertinent. For, assuming that the arrogances of the
specialism in the group have been mastered and collegiality
established, there will still be a tendency on the part of the group
to perseverate, to maintain attention on the one cluster of values
which, for whatever reason, has initially interested the group
at the start of one of its meetings. It is this perserveration which
the chairman must interrupt. His task is to see to it that the
deliberations of the group be appropriately saltatory, jumpy;
that it leave consideration of the affective value to the child,
for example, and consider the value of putative effects of the

curriculum bit on parents, on the finances of the operation, on the personality of the school principal, and so on. (Of course, the clusters of values left behind are revisited — again and again. The aim is not to make the deliberations less than thorough but to ensure juxtaposition of incommensurables so that they will, indeed, be weighed against one another.)

Two penultimate words. The two subphases described here — the generation of alternatives, the consideration of alternatives — do not follow one another in strict seriality. Obviously, there must be alternatives to consider. Hence some must be generated before the second subphase can be entered upon. But the deliberations involved in the second subphase are themselves rich sources of invention of new alternatives. The moments when such flashes of invention occur to a member of the group must be immediately honored, however important the considerations under discussion may appear to be.

The second penultimate word: neither of the subphases ends when the planning group has agreed on the curriculum bits it proposes to sponsor. The processes of invention and choice run on through the operations of evaluation earlier described and especially in that aspect of the evaluation which involves confrontation of the planning group with the untoward responses of the children themselves to the sponsored curriculum bit.

A last word. The device of confrontation referred to above is one way in which the child can enter the curricular discussion, speak for himself. Other devices toward the same end — and with reference to the teacher and the community as well as the child — should be sought.

NOTES

1. This chapter, in modified form, appears as *The Practical 3: Translation into Curriculum* in *School Review,* August 1973, pp. 501-522.

2. Edited by Hollis Summers, Boston: D.C. Health and Company, 1963.

3. James E. Miller. Jr., in *The Bulletin of the National Association of Secondary School Principals,* April 1967, no. 318.

2

TRANSLATING JEWISH HISTORY INTO CURRICULUM
From Scholarship to *Paideia* — A Case Study

Gerson D. Cohen

"Are you searching for something?" Lector Meir Friedman challenged young scholars in the library of the Bet Ha-Midrash of Vienna. "If so, you will, in all likelihood, discover something of interest and scholarly value, albeit not necessarily what you wanted or expected. But if you are not seeking something definite, you will read — and, of course, remember — much, but really learn precious little." Although basically an antiquarian and editor of classical rabbinic texts, Friedman reflected an insight into the meaning and process of genuine education that is particularly apposite to the problem of mediating the Jewish past to the American student of the twentieth century.

While any delimitation of the goals of the study of history is not only as futile as it is presumptuous, the pertinence of a knowledge of some history, at least to the non-professional historian, is surely dependent on, and considerably determined by, the overall goal of the education that any given group seeks to impart to its constituents, young as well as mature. The physician may well forego some of the historic awareness that the corporate executive will need for his work and still function responsibly and intelligently in the processes of inquiry and decision-making which are the obligation of the general citizenry for the healthy functioning of a democratic society such as ours. The political functionary or civil servant will require relatively greater competence in certain areas of history which the average citizen — corporate executive, physician, clergyman, and so on — will not normally be called upon to reflect. But fundamental to all of them will be a familiarity with a certain body of historical data generally acknowledged to be indispensable to responsible and intelligent citizenship and some methodological training in weighing of evidence and in gauging the relative importance of varying historical considerations. If part of the process of education is the awakening of the student to his roots — which will thus clarify and deepen his awareness of himself in the context of the various groups into which fate and (later on, possibly) personal choice have thrust him — a second, and perhaps equally important, element in an open and politically free society is an appreciation of the process of inquiry by which the past has been reconstructed and (inevitably) evaluated as well as a recognition of the tentative nature of these findings and appraisals. Most important, the very awakening and deepening of self-awareness through a confrontation with the past will inevitably be oriented by the underlying assumptions of what the matured "self" should be or should aspire to become. This function of the study of the past is as true for a society hell-bent on breaking with all precedent and transmitted values as for a society that is intransigent in its insistence on keeping the legacy of the past perfectly intact and reproducing itself to the exclusion of any influences from outside its physical or spiritual fortress. In short, history is a major component in orienting the citizen to preserving and transmitting or to modifying and restructuring the cultural matrix of his society.

History as a Component of *Paideia*

The inevitable conclusion to these considerations is that history serves as an indispensible component of *paideia*. What we take to be the goal of education generally and the way we construe the image of the ideal citizen will largely determine the way in which we study the past, search for data in it, mediate the results of our inquiry, and train others to evaluate the accepted data on the past and any new information that may turn up.

In a fundamental way, it seems to me, the cultural pains that we are today experiencing in educational institutions on all levels are the consequences and reflection of a loss of confidence in the traditional conceptions of *paideia* that have determined our curricula — be they of the Roman Catholic, humanist, or modernized religious types — and of the tensions between residual cultural configurations of varying strength on the one hand, and of new ideals being advocated with varying degrees of aggressiveness, on the other, which, whatever their nature, require the overhauling of traditional institutions, curricula, standards of judgment, and methods of instruction. To a considerable degree the tension is between those who know what they want out of education, even in a general way, and those who are not orienting their education to any goal.

Moreover, if educational institutions provide any index of the current cultural temper, what the authorities determining the structure and orientation of educational institutions seem to have lost is the connective thread between the various components of formal education. It is of no import whatever whether the components of formal education in previous generations really dovetailed into a structure that expressed the dominant notion of the purposes of education. It is enough that most were willing to accept the system as though it reflected an integrated synthesis of skills and knowledge propaedeutic to social and intellectual maturity. Whatever consensus obtained, at least in official or representative institutions, is now lost or at the very least a bone of heated contention. The relation of history to literature and of both of these to science, philosophy, religion, and civic maturity is no longer even acknowledged, let alone understood.

Of vital importance in the teaching of meaningful cultural history — and to be quite blunt, our generation has frequently failed to impart to students a firm conviction on the importance of such history — is the necessity of imparting the connection in any given time and place between the various components of society and the regnant conception of *paideia*. When this is lacking, history deteriorates into a jumble of dates and events, for the would-be historian or teacher of history has failed to achieve himself and, accordingly, to communicate to his audience, connective thread between various components of the past that are being examined and "learned." At the risk of being repetitive, I must emphasize that this diagnosis and implied guideline for educational planning should not be construed as an effort to restrict unfettered research and original approaches to the teaching of any subject, and most specifically, in this context, of history. The study of the past needs no rationale, and the interpretation and teaching of the past require no more validation beyond the requirements of precision, dispassionate study, and intellectual honesty. But we are not discussing scientific inquiry or scholarship *per se*. Our attention is focused on history as part of a total curriculum and as an element in the total fabric of education. Now, if education is to be a strong fabric, some context is required and, however that context is construed, it will reflect, even unconsciously, some notion of *paideia*.

In the study and teaching of Jewish history, which is the immediate area of our concern, scholars of our time have harped on the need for a critical approach, so that, quite apart from any other considerations, the orientation of Jewish education should not be totally out of line with the universe of discourse in which Jews are educated for life as a whole. Great stress has been laid on the need to alert the student to an understanding of Jewish history not reflected in dogmatic texts and, accordingly, to the need of bringing him to see uncensored data and to appraising Jewish political, economic, social, intellectual, and religious development in the light of the general milieu in which the Jews lived. To cite but two examples out of countless instances that could be adduced, modern biblical and talmudic research have demonstrated that it is impossible to understand and evaluate biblical and rabbinic culture critically without reference to Near Eastern culture or Hellenistic civilization of which the ancient people of Israel and the Jews were but a small part. To put the matter differently, a critical study of the Bible and of rabbinic literature will explicate these bodies of literature and sources of historical knowledge as aspects and particular expressions of the ancient Near Eastern and Hellenistic civilizations in which they sprouted. Biblical society was a Near Eastern society, and the Israelites a Near Eastern people. Rabbinic leaders and commentators were Hellenistic leaders and commentators, rabbinic religion a Hellenistic one.

Needless to say, the task of the teacher of Jewish history has its own challenges and complications. The teacher of Jewish history is expected to explain what befell the Jews and how Jews reacted in the light of: (1) the general historic milieu and (2) the particular drives and legacies motivating the Jews to respond. The historian is thus called upon to elucidate the features of Jewish life common to other peoples of their time and place and, simultaneously, the uniqueness of Jewish behavior and the continuity of Jewish history. However, to distinguish one segment of Jewish history from any other, it is not enough to explain the external forces shaping Jewish behavior and development. Nor is it sufficient to show how Jews responded to these challenges. What is required above all is a clear formulation of the changing syntheses that the Jewish leadership developed at any particular time and place as these became expressed in a new conception of *paideia,* or of the ideal Jew, and to relate these syntheses to the "external forces" shaping the Jewish community and its ideals. (Not always, to be sure, did Jews develop such new syntheses, but when they failed to do so, as for example, in Ottoman areas after the Sabbatian debacle, their civilization declined and soon became fossilized.)

Such a construction, I believe, provides a specific and meaningful context for Jewish history which, because of its peculiar characteristics, is so frequently compartmentalized and dismissed by the student as quite unrelated to any other form of historical experience he has studied and as totally irrelevant to his own cultural context. Indeed, since Jewish history is by its very nature so different from the history of other peoples and institutions (which have the obvious advantages of geographic, linguistic, and political-institutional circumscription, and consequently of intelligibility) that some connective thread — for Jewish history itself and between the history of other Jewish groups and that of the American Jew — is crucial if the subject matter is to provide some insight into the problems of Jewish identity, Jewish continuity, and the nature of Jewish culture. Such a specific thread is particularly necessary in the

United States where corporate Jewish life and experience —
social, political, and cultural — have had to be forged almost
de novo and virtually with no model or precedent in Jewish
history.

Given the uniqueness of the American Jewish situation
in terms of Jewish history, we must decide whether we can
speak with conviction and intelligence of American Jewish
history in and of itself, and as a link in the chain of Jewish
history as a whole. If not, then we may abandon the study of
Jewish history to antiquarians and remove it from the agenda
of those concerned with Jewish education. But if even in
America Jewish history continues, and thus reflects some connective thread with earlier Jewish experience (and with the
experiences of other contemporary Jewish communities), the
study of Jewish history becomes vital, even if frequently only
largely as a focus for contrast.

Since our concern with Jewish education and a Jewish
curriculum implies the desirability in our eyes of a corporate
Jewish identity in the United States, of a relationship of
American Jews with other Jewries, past as well as present,
and of a way of life that can only be attained by a discrete form
of education that American society as a whole will entertain,
but not provide, the history of the Jews must be related to
American Jewish life and experience; that is, this history must
suggest some continuing thread, some constant Jewish quest
for corporate expression.

We suggest that one such connective and continuing thread
is the history of Jewish *paideia* which, among other things,
has the virtue of being the consequence of conscious Jewish
efforts at creativity and response to external circumstance.
This connective thread has the further virtue of being intimately
related to Jewish education in the United States. For, if Jewish

education is to produce any significant yield in this country, it will have to be at the least a Jewish response to American society that will constitute a peculiarly American Jewish synthesis and dialect of the Jewish experience, tradition, and value-complex. This will require the rewriting of Jewish history to bring its relevance home to the Jewish student and to achieve for the American Jew what we feel the study of history in our society seeks to achieve generally.

What follows, then, is a case study that serves as a sample of how Jewish history may be taught in keeping with these considerations. No effort and certainly no claim is implied for the definitiveness of our construction and interpretation. Indeed, even if it should be found to be scientifically sound and winsome in its reasoning, we would hope that the tentativeness of its structure, evaluation, and conclusions would be assumed part of the presentation. It goes without saying that for the sake of brevity, we have omitted even the kind of documentation — such as texts and documents in translation — that we think should be a regular part of the fare of any historical study, even on the most elementary level. The study of the period we shall describe has been immeasurably enriched through recent discoveries of documents and the scientific editing and analysis of classical texts. These tools will be totally taken for granted in this discussion, although they should not be in the classroom. What we propose here is a series of specific and connective threads which will yield a recognition of a form of Jewish *paideia* and of the historic consideration that underlay this quest for an ideal Jew.

"Our Crowd" of Andalus: 1000-1148

As anyone with even the most superficial contact with Jewish culture knows, European Jewish communities were

generally classified as members of two broad subgroups known
as Ashkenazim and Sephardim, Ashkenazim generally being
translated as German, and Sephardim generally being applied
to Jews of Spanish-Portuguese extraction. Now while with
respect to specific issues or institutions it is more accurate to
subdivide European Jewry into smaller subcategories such as
Italian, Provençal, French, German, Levantine, Romaniotes,
and so forth, it is nevertheless true that these two basic divisions
of European Jewry into Germanic and Hispanic serve to describe
the cultural, religious, and social heritages of the two dominant
branches of European/Jewish culture.

These two groups are easily distinguishable by many
characteristic features of which the most noticeable is the dif-
ference in Hebrew pronunciation, Ashkenazic and Sephardic.
To the specialist, they are also distinguished from each other
by different rituals, different study habits, different attitudes
even toward basic doctrines of faith and, further, by characteristic occupational distribution, at least in the Middle Ages.

One peculiar characteristic of Sephardic culture and community life that is frequently mentioned but unexplained is the
view advanced by the Sephardim of themselves that they
constitute not only an ethnic subgroup — or "nation" as they
called themselves — but that they also constituted a distinct
social class, indeed an aristocracy. The Sephardim spoke of
themselves uninhibitedly as an elite entitled to special deference
and treatment by Jews and Gentiles alike. In many communities,
for example, Turkey, Italy, Holland, Europe, England, and
even in the United States, the Sephardim often preferred to
have their daughters remain spinsters than see them married
to Ashkenazim. Everywhere, Sephardim maintained their own
synagogues and communal administration. To this day in
London, Amsterdam, and New York the Spanish-Portuguese

Jewish federations conduct their own charity networks and retain at least a nominal separation from the remainder of the organized Jewish community. However quaint such separatism may appear today, it has recently begun to enjoy a renaissance even in the United States and, of course, in Israel, at least in religious and cultural pursuits. Israel has not one Chief Rabbi but two, a Sephardi and an Ashkenazi.

Now this posture was maintained not only within the Jewish community but in relations with Gentiles as well. Perhaps the most notorious instance is the one that occurred on December 24, 1789, when the French National Constituent Assembly considered the possibility of granting the Jews of France rights as citizens. The Assembly was immediately presented with a petition from the Jews of Bordeaux, who expressed deep chagrin that the question of *their* emancipation could be lumped together with that of the Jews of Alsace-Lorraine. After all, the Jews of Bordeaux, they said, had always been regarded by the kings of France as a separate nation, by which of course they meant, if I may employ modern jargon, an ethnic subgroup with its own political as well as social precedents.

This claim to special status actually goes a long way back and could be duplicated by many instances, one of which is truly pathetic. In the fifteenth century, when many Jews in Spain converted to Christianity, some of the spokesmen of these New Christians claimed special privileges even as Christians. While it is true, they said, that baptism makes men equal in Christ, temporally some men were more privileged than others, and they should not be treated quite on the same plane even within the Church. For example, they argued, no one would presume to say that a prince who converted to Christianity should be treated with the same temporal respect that is accorded to a peasant or a burgher. Obviously, we treat princes as princes and accord them the more honor once they have become Christians. In view of the native nobility of these New Christians, who were for the most part descended from noble Jewish stock and therefore socially far superior to the average Spaniard, they were to be treated, they said, one and all as Spanish aristocracy. Their conversion had not erased their native exalted station.

Now it is pointless to dismiss these public expressions as mere propaganda and Iberian Jewish vanity. The question is, of course, where Spanish Jews got such notions about themselves. Clearly, these claims were part of a collective Sephardic memory and they must be explained. Happily, there is considerable evidence to allow us to trace the growth, if not the actual origin, of this mentality.

To do this, we have to go back to the roots of Sephardic culture in Andalus, as the Jews called Arab Spain, shortly before the year 1000 when a series of ostensibly discrete but basically related Jewish phenomena occurred in the city of Cordova and its environs.

First, there was the sudden and dramatic rise of Jews to high political office in the service of the Arab caliphs. Three outstanding examples of such attainment are particularly striking. Hisdai ibn Shaprut of the city of Cordova served as a courtier under Abd ar-Rahman III and his son Ali Hakim approximately between the years 960 and 990. Samuel ibn Nagrela, known in Hebrew as Samuel ha-Nagid, and his son Joseph were both viziers, or prime ministers, of the petty kingdom of Granada between the years 1030 and 1066. At the same time that the Ibn Nagrelas were functioning in Cordova and held power there, a lesser know Jewish vizier by the name of Abu-'l-Fadl ibn Hisdai functioned in Saragossa. While it is true that in the early day of the Reconquista Jews held significant political posts in Spanish Christian society, they never held quite as important positions there and certainly never rose to the policy-making status that they attained in Arabic society. It was only in the south, under the Muslims, that the Jews really became policy makers and wielders of the reins of government.

Why should the Arabs have permitted the Jews to rise to such distinction? Actually, it should never be overlooked that official Arab doctrine decried power in the hands of Jews no less than Christian doctrine did. Jewish political attainment cannot be attributed to greater tolerance of Islam for infidels. While many explanations have been offered, a plausible reason for this dramatic reversal of posture toward Jews on the part of the Arabs of Spain was that in a country where the Arab rulers were always a minority, the Jews were a trustworthy — or relatively trustworthy — group, for they alone had no vested interests in any particular political configuration of Spain. Within Muslim circles, for example, there were constant tensions between various Arab clans on the one hand, and between Arabs and non-Arab Muslims, principally Berbers, on the other. Christians could not, of course, be trusted by the Arabs, for they were under suspicion of loyalty to the kings of the north, and therefore suspected of having an interest in driving the Arabs out of the Iberian peninsula. The Jews alone appeared to be above partisan interest and could presumably be relied on to serve their masters faithfully and without any reservation.

Though even in Muslim Spain the Jews for the most part did not rise to supreme positions except after the break-up of the Caliphate (ca. 1013), nevertheless, even before that time they were often charged with very delicate and trustworthy assignments. According to plausible, but unverifiable, reports, the Arabs had even appointed the Jews as local political and financial administrators soon after their conquest of the Iberian peninsula in the eighth century. Christians, accordingly, later accused the Jews of having facilitated the conquest of Spain by the Muslims, although this claim does not rest on any documentary evidence. In any event, the Jews did enjoy a long period of governmental service under the Arabs of Spain from the outset of Muslim control of the peninsula.

But the Jewish exercise of political power became conspicuous when the Muslims of Spain broke away from the eastern Caliphate and established an independent Arab empire in the west. The Arabs looked even more to the Jews as a particularly trustworthy ethnic group whose services were more vital than ever. The trustworthiness of the Jews was coupled with a second asset, and that was that the Jews of Spain had international connections with fellow Jews. They had very old traditions of travel and commercial activity and were frequently bilingual or trilingual. This has been dramatically documented for us in recent years through the science of papyrology which has shown that Jews and Syrian traders were well known as international travelers and merchants. Since the Arabs of the west, after their break with the eastern Caliphate, were desperately in need of talented and trusted couriers and civil servants both in Spain and elsewhere, the Jews suited their needs very well. In other words, not Muslim tolerance but Muslim *need* opened new doors to talented Jews.

But the Arabs were at the same time a discriminating group who claimed cultural superiority over all other groups and would only show respect to those who could boast their own cultural attainments in the fields that Arabs respected. Hence in imitation of the Arabs, Jewish men of wealth and political influence on the Iberian peninsula began to cultivate their own petty court poets, linguists, philosophers, and scientists. Spain is notorious for the rise of the Jewish Maecenas, the Jewish philanthropist who patronized culture by giving personal and private handouts to his favorites who showed talents in the field of writing and scholarship. The result was that between the years 1000 and 1200 Spain enjoyed a golden age of Hebrew literature that still dazzles scholars by its sheer beauty, variety, and originality.

The Jews of Andalus readily acknowledged that their cultivation of new areas of study — Hebrew linguistics, Hebrew poetry, as well as astronomoy, mathematics, and philosophy, about which they wrote in Arabic — had been stimulated by the intellectuals of the Muslim society. Since the Arabs themselves regarded intellectual life as a major component of political and especially of court activity, the Jews began to try to excel in new areas — quite apart from the rabbinic ones which they shared with other Jewish communities — and thus came to the attention of their Muslim overlords. The consequence was the growth of a new type of Jewish literature and of a new type of Jewish intellectual. So proud indeed did Jews become of their new intellectual attainments, that they even began to reflect on the history of their development as a distinctive Jewish group of Spain who, in imitation of the Arabs again, terminated their independence on the rabbis and academies of Babylonia for religious and cultural guidance.

The Andalusian Jews divided their cultural history into four periods. The first, from 960 to 980, the days of Ibn Shaprut, they considered the infancy of their renaissance. From 980 to 1020 they began to produce the new literature that was modelled after Arabic literature. Maturation began, they said, 1020-1050, when the Ibn Nagrelas controlled Granada and became the dominant figures in Jewish culture. Then finally came the golden age from 1050 to 1148, which was terminated by the violent invasion of the Almohades.

The real heyday of Jewish creativity developed as a consequence of the policy of the Ibn Nagrelas and their Jewish competitors in dispensing wealth, friendship, and influence to encourage the rise of a *native* Spanish-Jewish culture. I emphasize the word "native," for the Jews of Spain were extremely sensitive to the fact that they were a distinctive Jewish community.

What were the fields they cultivated and for which they were willing to spend vast amounts of money in order to show themselves as well as the Arabs they were a creative and superior cultural group? First and foremost, as the world soon noticed, Hebrew poetry. From the fourth period of Andalusian Jewish development alone we know of some fifty poets of distinction of whom we need mention only a few of the more famous ones: Solomon ibn Gabirol, Moses ibn Ezra, Judah Halevi. Since the politicians held poetry in esteem and dispensed rewards for achievement in that area, poetry became the popular Jewish fad. From Ibn Ezra we know that it was the common fashion for Jews to gather at a home, have some wine, and conduct a poetic contest — extemporaneous or prepared.

But here we come to the paradox of this new Hebraic culture which expressed itself in poetry. The Jews of Spain revived the writing of poetry in biblical Hebrew. In other words they glossed over the intervening stages of Hebrew, talmudic and early medieval Hebrew, and went back to original, classical, biblical Hebrew. But paradoxially they set that biblical Hebrew to Arabic meter, which is fundamentally alien to the structure of the Hebrew language. Since they wrote in biblical terms they naturally wrote liturgical poetry in imitation of the Psalms. But they did not stop there. They did not only sing of God and of the chosen people and of the revelation. They wrote of wine, women, song, and pretty little boys. They mused about the scenery, about politics, and about persons of distinction. In beautiful verse they wrote appeals for handouts and protests against insult.

All of this, of course, was in the fashion of Arabic tastes. Closely allied to poetry, naturally, was precision in language and that meant, therefore, biblical exegesis and philology. In the eleventh century, Judah ibn Hayyuj and Jonah ibn Janah laid the foundations for the science of Hebrew grammar and discovered, by comparison with Arabic, the tri-literal foundation of the Hebrew language. To this day their philological discoveries serve as a foundation for the study of Hebrew grammar.

What is more, as a result of the study of language and critical analysis of linguistic structure, they laid the foundations for biblical criticism. Moses ibn Gikatilla, Judah ibn Bala'am, and Abraham ibn Ezra are the fathers of what we call both lower and higher critcism. They not only ventured to suggest corrections in the structure of words in the Bible, but they even noted that parts of the Bible could not be dated at the time that some biblical books were purported to have been written. In other words, these three men anticipated Benedict de Spinoza's *Tractatus Theologico Politicus* by some 500 years. I mention this since Spinoza himself, by his footnotes, indicates that he had really been trained in his early doubts about the Bible by reading what these men had written. It was therefore from his Sephardic culture that Spinoza imbibed the roots of his criticism and his rationalism. Theirs was thus a very rational and critical approach even to sacred texts.

Rationalism and criticism are of course connected to a third field in which Andalusian Jewry distinguished itself — namely, philosophy. Solomon ibn Gabirol wrote a neo-Platonic treatise on faith in Arabic called *The Fountain of Life,* which was so universalist in tone that the nature of its true author was soon forgotten. Indeed, it was soon assumed that the author was a Christian who could be nominated for sainthood. Only a century and a quarter ago the world was shocked to learn that Avicebrol was neither an Arab nor a Christian, but a Jew by the name of Solomon ibn Gabirol. Clearly, he wrote philosophy in a way that never at any point betrayed its Jewish origin.

To turn to more distinctively Jewish works of philosophy, Bahya ibn Paquda synthesized Muslim Kalam and proto-Sufism with Judaism. Abraham ibn Daud, who is probably to be identified with the famous Jewish translator of Toledo, Avendauth, became the first distinguished Jewish Aristotelian of the Peninsula, and he may well have been the intermediary by which Aristotelianism came to Christian scholars in northern Spain. Judah Halevi's anti-philosophic *Book of the Kuzari* betrayed a tremendous training and knowledge of all of philosophic literature. Finally there came the last of this group of scholars, who wrote after the period was over, but who provided an epitaph and the apogee to this culture in many fields, Moses Maimonides' *Guide of the Perplexed*. Maimonides had been trained in Cordova and he betrayed a Cordovan orientation in everything he wrote.

Closely related to the field of philosophy were the fields of mathematics, medicine, and logic, which these Jews made part of their Jewish curricula in their academies of learning.

Apart from their role in the history of Western thought, as Etienne Gilson and Harry A. Wolfson have shown, these works of highly cultural character are of crucial interest for our study of Jewish history for several reasons. First, these men not only broadened the scope of Jewish knowledge and Jewish interests. What they actually did was to redefine Jewish faith and religious experience under the impact of Greek thought which they had imbibed via Arabic translation. The men I have mentioned were familiar with Plato and Aristotle, with Hippocrates and Galen, with Avicenna and Avempace, and could quote them as readily as they did the Bible, the Talmud, the Midrash, or the Hebrew liturgy. They represented, therefore, a new stage in the Hellenization of Judaism, for they really tried to bridge and synthesize Athens and Jerusalem.

What is of greatest interest is that all these men — politicians, poets, philologists, rabbis — were members of the same social class. And while they lived in half a dozen places, they always gravitated to Cordova as the center of their activity. With the decline of Cordova after 1013, they established an academy at a small town 35 miles southeast of it in Lucena, where they sent all their favorite sons to be trained. Any reader of the poems, chronicles, and scholarly rabbinic works that they produced immediately must come to the conclusion that they constituted a kind of "our crowd." In the first place, they celebrated each other. They fought one another with passionate sibling rivalry. They dispensed money together: thanks to the discoveries of Shlomo Dov Goitein, we now have some circular letters of appeal, a kind of United Andalusian Appeal for concerted Jewish causes. They cultivated the same subjects. One can almost identify a graduate of Lucena and of Cordova, for inevitably, he not only knows Talmud and Bible well; he writes poetry, or rhymed prose, philosophy, philology, and finally eschatology or speculation on the end of time and the date of the messianic redemption. When they moved to faraway cities because of politics or economic needs, they were forever writing to each other about every matter under the sun, whether it was politics, philanthropy, Jewish law, or even wine, women, and beauty.

Now the simple association of men and companionship makes perhaps for a crowd — even a coterie — but not necessarily an "our crowd" in the sense that Birmingham has made the phrase a technical one and as these men immediately were. By "our crowd" I mean a group with a common *Weltanschauung* and a common purpose. And it is this common bond that distinguished the Jews of Andalus, and particularly of the Cordovan center from 1050 to 1148, from every other Jewish group in the Middle Ages. It is their common vision and way of life that need to be defined, for they will explain these and many other symptomatic features of Sephardic culture, such as those I mentioned at the outset of our discussion.

What motivated this element and the twelfth-century renaissance of the Jews of Andalus, as I have indicated, was the stimulus, the encouragement, and the competition of the dominant Arab rulers and their culture. The Jews copied them and vied with them. But closer inspection of this culture of the Jews will reveal that it was not mere copying and not outright imitation. It was a very purposeful adaption for two reasons and purposes.

First, the Arabs considered literary polish a prerequisite for diplomatic training and service. Elegance and cleverness of expression were vital in their eyes for anyone who was going to be entrusted with a diplomatic or governmental post. Many an Arab ruler and diplomat boasted that he had risen to power by virtue of his poetry or literary expertise. The Arabs, therefore, expected the same of their underlings. The famous Al-Mansur claimed that he had been elevated to power simply because he had written letters and poetry so well. And the Jews told the identical story of Samuel ibn Nagrela. According to the Jewish version, Samuel had been languishing as a spice merchant in a shop in Malaga where he had occasion to write letters for servants of the vizier of Granada, and it was in that way that he was discovered and appointed to a diplomatic post from which he rose to the vizierate. Modern scholarship has shown that it is an unlikely story. Indeed, it was probably as untrue of Al-Mansur as it was of Ibn Nagrela. But it was a very interesting kind of legend that was intelligible to the audience, for it represented a typological ideal of rise to power, not through a knowledge or political science or even of the military arts but through a mastery of Arabic rhetoric.

Since literature and writing were so intimately connected with power, the literary and scholarly debates that we have from the period of "our crowd" of Andalus are not scholarly reviews. They read like political vendettas; and indeed they had political consequences. For example, Hisdai ibn Shaprut had a court poet Menahem ben Saruq, who wrote verses for his master on a variety of subjects — in praise of his master and on various other subjects. But along came a North African Jew from Fez, a man by the name of Dunash, who showed a new tendency in poetry — the ability to set Hebrew poetry to Arabic meter — and Menahem not only lost his stipend, but was thrown into prison as a consequence of the jealousy of his rival. Needless to say, the imprisonment was grounded on the charge of heresy, treason, and whatnot. But that will not really bear up under examination as far as the documents in the dispute indicate. What was important here was that poetry was a vehicle of power and a key to fellowship and "fellowships."

Samuel ibn Nagrela, vizier of Granada, wrote a violent diatribe against Judah ibn Hayyuj because the latter did not regard Samuel ibn Nagrela's treatises on the structure of the language philologically correct. More than philology was at stake here. If Ibn Nagrela's knowledge of the Hebrew language could be questioned, then perhaps he was not as astute a diplomat as he should be. Now by our canons of thinking this is a *non sequitur*. But Ibn Nagrela was hysterical about grammatical works that came from counter schools, for culture was all important and was a vehicle to power.

For the same reason presumably Abraham ibn Daud wrote with absolutely blind fury against the neo-Platonists and especially against Solomon ibn Gabirol. Philosophy was one of the vehicles for control of Jewish communal machinery.

The first clue, then, to the riddle of Jewish culture in Spain was the fact that Arabs stimulated it; Jews could gain some recognition only by having a cultural aristocracy of their own. But there was another side to the coin. The Jews did not only write in Arabic and show their expertise in Arabic language; they did so in Hebrew as well. To the Jews, self-pride required adapting and synthesizing Arabic culture with their own Hebraic culture to show the Arabs and their own people that the world of Jacob was as rich and as colorful and therefore as creative as that of Ishmael. They had to reaffirm their own faith in the face of the challenge of Hellenistic and Arabic philosophy. And they had to reaffirm their faith in the power of their sacred tongue in the face of the language of the Quran and the later Arabic poets.

The Arabs often claimed half seriously, but not totally jocosely, that they conquered the world with the magic power of their language. The Jews conceded this claim, and they often maintained that the Arabs displayed their power through the magic of their poetry and the magic of their prose as well. They also claimed that Hebrew was potentially equally powerful and that the Jews could, therefore, have their own renaissance if they could discover the wellsprings of energy and vitality of Hebrew poetry.

Indeed, some Christians of Cordova also adopted this line. Eulogius and Alvarro of the ninth century tried to revive Latin poetry and knowledge of Latin among Christians of Cordova. They failed for a variety of reasons, not the least of which was that the Arabs were not too encouraging to the Christians. In any event, since the Arabic language was the language of the Muslim Scripture, the Jews tried to recreate the poetry of the Psalms of David and the wisdom of Solomon in their classical and sacred tongue.

Once some of them attained power through the power of language and of philosophy, they began to dream and muse of other pristine glories. Perhaps the Jews again could be princes and soldiers, rulers and conquerers, priests and nobles. It was not a wild dream. After all, Samuel ibn Nagrela was not only a vizier, a Talmudist and a poet; he also became Commander-in-Chief of the armies of Granada and functioned in that capacity successfully.

At this point the Spanish Jews began to revive an old myth that was handy for their propaganda. They were, they said, genealogically worthy of exalted station for they were descendents not of all Jews of ancient Palestine, but of the nobility of Jerusalem, of the house of David, from the seed of Judah, and, here I quote two writers of the golden age, "they were not Jews from towns, unwalled cities and villages." They had then the blood of the aristocracy. That is why, they modestly conceded, their Hebrew poetry was more beautiful than any other Hebrew poetry that had been written since biblical times. Hence they began to write in terms that will occasionally sound to us megalomaniacal. But to them these terms were ideals and goals, sometimes very real ones in their eyes. Ibn Negrela actually could say: "I am the David of my generation." He meant not only a David in terms of poetry (which he did, though quite mistakenly by modern tastes) but he meant also David as a conqueror, and there he was not so mistaken. He meant also

a man who would someday restore ancient Jewish power and
revive the glories of the ancient past.

Consider some of the ways in which Hisdai ibn Shaprut's
versifiers addressed him and you realize that Ibn Nagrela did
not create his poetic fantasies out of whole cloth. Here is what
a poet wrote to Ibn Shaprut long before Samuel ibn Nagrela
came on the scene:

> Lily of the valleys (Song of Songs 2.1)
> Ever-opened blossom (Ibid. 7.13)
> Who shines like the gold
> Of the frontlet on Aaron's brow (Ex. 28.36, 38)
> Generous and firm,
> When you begin to shine,
> The ends of the earth
> Broke forth into song. (Isa. 49.13)

Or again:

> Attired in honor and glory (Ezek. 24.17)
> Clothed with divine salvation (Ps. 132.16)
> Seeking the good of his people
> He caused their enemies to scatter. (Est. 10.3)

Each phrase in these verses comes from a biblical context,
from the Song of Songs, from Ezekiel, the Book of Esther.
And now comes a poem that was considered one of the best
examples of how to address a person in terms of his just deserts,
a poem written by Joseph ibn Hisdai of Saragossa to Samuel ibn
Nagrela around the year 1050:

> Prince unique is R. Samuel
> Whose name has filled the earth.
> As a tower it has risen over the people of Israel,
> Established aloft as a fort for his nation.
> Through him was renewed for his sacred tribe

A seat of honor above the starry heavens.
This Samuel is none other than the Samuel of yore
Who had been summoned to enter the Temple of God.
Who knows, indeed, but that he has been
    magically revived
To rise from the dead, body and soul.
And if, indeed, that is not the case,
In their righteousness complete, they are none
    but the same.

This was the function for which the courtiers of "our crowd" cultivated writers to write for them. They regarded themselves as *Sarim, Nesiim* and *Negidim,* terms identifying them as princes and kings, and they spoke of themselves always as *zera ha-Misrah,* the royal line of rule.

They could even explain how it had happened that they had attained such heights; indeed, they could even date the event. When Titus conquered Jerusalem in the year 70 and announced his victory throughout the Roman world, the governor of Spain requested the Romans to provide as a gift a specimen of the finest aristocracy of Judea whom he could display in triumph. Titus accordingly sent an ancestor of the Ibn al-Balia family who was settled in Merida where he begat descendents. This nobility reproduced itself so that Spain was full of the only authentic remnants of the House of David and the nobility of Jerusalem in Europe.

In this connection, it is interesting to trace the change in the self-image advanced by the Andalusians. In the latter part of the ninth century, the Jews of Spain had liked to be addressed as descendants of the first exile from Judea to Babylonia in the days of Nebuchadnezzar. But in the eleventh century, when "our crowd" represented itself as seed of the house of David, they preferred to be addressed as descendants of the

Second Exile, for they could then trace their noble role in the Holy Land right back to the final days of Jerusalem in the days of the Second Temple.

This vision of nobility and culture dovetailed with another sentiment which the Arab rulers also encouraged. That was religious nativism. In earlier times the Jews of Spain had been dependent on the rabbis and academies of Iraq, Baghdad, and Babylonia, as the Arabs had turned to scholars and religious leaders in the East. In earlier days, the Jews of Spain were accustomed to send contributions and religious questions to the academies in Babylonia and in return they received responsa and whole books which were written at their request. But under the stimulus of the new Western caliphate, the Jews began to assert their own religious autonomy against the religious hegemony of the Jews of Babylonia.

Of course they rationalized their change in behavior with several interesting stories, none of which are historical. The first is the famous study of the four captives which has become one of the more popular Jewish stories of medieval origin. A second story, which has not yet been published, is a story of a threat from Palestinian academies to the Jews of Cordova that unless the latter sent their questions to Palestine, they would be excommunicated. The Cordovans are said to have replied with utter contempt. Again, that story too was circulated to indicate that the Jews of Spain had become religiously autonomous.

But they did not content themselves with tendentious stories. Samuel ibn Nagrela wrote a series of tracts to show that in talmudic knowledge he was superior to the head of the Academy of Baghdad, who was acknowledged to be the Gaon or religious prince of world Jewry. Once again Ibn Nagrela's real concern was not religious theory, but one of power: the Jews of Spain, he indicated, had the right of religious codification, without recourse to Babylonia. Isaac al-Fasi, whose name shows that he was a foreigner, came to Spain from North Africa and tried to get a position there. He was at first bitterly opposed by "our crowd." For a long time he could not find a home until he was adopted by the aristocracy and given a post in the Academy of Lucena. There he immediately set about serving the needs of "our crowd" and issued a new code of Jewish law which became famous as an abridged Talmud. This was a major act of daring on the part of a medieval Jew — to write a new version of the Talmud, as it were, in which he very plainly indicated that in many instances the Babylonian precedent was not to be followed and that Spanish rabbis had independent access to religious knowledge and at least expertise with the Babylonians. In 1161 Abraham ibn Daud issued a chronicle in which he espoused the same theory saying that the Gaonate, or religious headship of Babylonia, had come to an end and that its rightful and legitimate successor was the Rabbinate of Spain. I should indicate that Ibn Daud even invented a new term, the Rabbinate, which begins with him, for until that time there was no such term. He thus tried to create a new kind of religious and political category that served the needs of the "crowd" of which he was a member.

Finally, between 1155 and 1165, Moses Maimonides, now an exile from Spain but still very much part of the Cordovan crowd, denied that the great religious leaders of Babylonia, the heads of the Academies of Baghdad, were to be accorded any more respect than any local judge. Every little judge or *dayyan,* as we call them in Hebrew, was to be accorded the same respect. He then re-defined the word "Gaon" to mean not the head of the Academy of Baghdad but any rabbi who came after the redaction of the Babylonian Talmud. In a word, the "crowd" of Cordova took its cue from its political leaders and grounded their claims in new religious theories. They had outgrown the mother community of Iraq and would now be subservient to no one. The Arabs, of course, were delighted with this, for in the first instance Jewish money that had previously been contributed to Babylonia now remained in Spain. Secondly, the Jews of Spain began to attract scholarly talent to their own shores rather than suffer a brain drain to the east, as had been the case in the ninth century. What had therefore begun as a tendentious plea soon became a social dogma.

From the chronicles of Ibn Daud and others we know that Spanish Jewry began to consider itself the true aristocracy and the true leadership of the Jewish people. It was this kind of sentiment that determined the *paideia* of the Andalusian leadership who saw the sudden collapse in 1148 of all Andalusian culture, through circumstances beyond their control.

The Almohade armies overran North Africa, crossed the Straits of Gibraltar, and within six months wiped out all of the Christian, Jewish, and unorthodox Muslim communities in the south of Spain. The Jews fled in all directions: Maimonides to Egypt, where he tried to start a new "our crowd" in Cairo and produced a body of theory designed to build again a new kind of autonomous society in Egypt; in the north, Jews fled to Toledo and tried to re-establish the same kind of society. But here they collided with an established old Ashkenazic type of Jewish community, and thus began a controversy in which two different Jewish *paideias* clashed tragically. The Maimunist controversy was presumably about philosophy, but really was about power and *paideia*. Nevertheless, the original Sephardic temper persisted in some circles, as we have seen, down to modern times.

All Andalusian education was oriented toward becoming Jewish aristocracy or serving it. Poetry, philosophy, science, linguistics, and critical analysis of sacred texts were not the product of mere Spanish Jewish genius. They were part of a program whose ultimate aim was religio-political.

Postscript

The nature of Andalusian Jewish *paideia* and the history of the Jews of Spain have been amply recounted in many works of scholarship. We have not intended to summarize them and certainly not to explain what made the period we have discussed "The Golden Age." What we have tried to argue is that what is frequently presented as a series of disjointed facts — often quite enchanting ones — take on a new significance when the *paideia* is selected as the connective thread of Jewish political posture and activity, economic station, and cultural adaptation (or isolation). What we have attempted for the Andalusian experience can easily be duplicated for the talmudic period, Ashkenazic societies, and modern Jewish Palestine and Israel.

Hopefully, the effort, if utilized in the classroom will stimulate teacher, student and communal leadership to study American Jewish behavior in the same way. Perhaps the American Jewish experience will become more intelligible. Perhaps someone will advance new and more inspiring forms of *paideia* and character-education for American Jewry so that Jewish education will cease to be an exercise merely in texts and liturgical skills.

3

TRANSLATING JEWISH THOUGHT INTO CURRICULUM
Moral Philosophy in Jewish Education

Marvin Fox

In this paper [1] I want to explore some specific ways in which the scholarly study of Jewish philosophy (and, for that matter, some themes in general philosophy) can make important contributions to Jewish educational practice. I begin with the assumption that Jewish education is more than a purely intellectual exercise, that it is concerned with helping the student come to terms with his own Jewishness, and that it aims also at making it possible for the student to remain a committed Jew in the context of contemporary society. Philosophical study is particularly important for these purposes, since Jewish philosophy, more than any other Jewish intellectual enterprise has usually arisen as a response to intellectual challenges posed by the cultures and civilizations in which the Jewish people found themselves. I am not suggesting that the formal study of philosophical texts as such has a place in the Jewish school, surely not in the elementary school and perhaps not even in the high school. What I do want to argue is that a scholarly understanding of the work of the philosophers can, and should, be translated into curricular elements for the Jewish school. To illustrate and defend this point I propose to take up a single major philosophical issue, to show how Jewish philosophers have dealt with it and to give some indications of how one might move from a sophisticated scholarly examination of this issue to its use in the school situation.

The Problem of Moral Choice

One of the most aggravated concerns of contemporary society, one from which the Jewish school surely must not hide itself, is the problem posed by moral choice and decision. We live in an age of moral relativism, while the Jewish tradition teaches a fixed and binding morality. The biblical text offers commandments and prohibitions, but hardly any theoretical guidance for the man who wants to think his way independently to a moral position.[2] In contrasting the virtue of believers who follow God's way with the abominations of the idolaters who are wicked and depraved, Scripture offers an ideal but not an argument. It only affirms that God has commanded us and that we are, by virtue of that fact alone, bound to observe his commandments. Rather than evidence that its commandments are truly good, Scripture persuades by the promise of rewards to those who fulfill the commandments and the threat of punishment to those who transgress them. This may be satisfying so long as one is not inclined to challenge the theoretical foundations on which this view is based. If one accepts without protest or critical reflection the claim that God alone is the source of our knowledge of right and wrong, and that He has made His teaching known to us in the canonical texts, then the traditional doctrine is sufficient. For the student there is left only the task of learning what it is that God commands him to do and of proceeding to maximize his capacity to follow the divine way which the official tradition has set out for him.

Even in a society favorably disposed to tradition such an approach to morality cannot satisfy the reflective man. It simply fails to take account of the complexities and subtleties of the moral life and the processes of moral choice. and decision. In an age of moral relativism or moral skepticism this traditional approach to the moral life is clearly insufficient. It can be taken for granted that thoughtful students will be unwilling merely to accept as an article of faith the established teaching concerning moral obligation. They have alternate models readily available to them, and these pose an inescapable challenge to the traditional way. Without the work of philosphical reflection on right and wrong, good and evil, we have no resources with which to help our students explore the basic issues and either come to a position of their own or recognize the validity of Jewish moral teaching. It is precisely at this point that the work of the philosophers takes on major importance for educational practice. By their very commitment as philosophers they must seek a rational analysis and justification of any position that they affirm. If, as is the case with major Jewish philosophers, they remain committed to the fixed norms of Jewish law, they can only do so after pursuing such rational analysis and providing the requisite rational justification. They cannot and do not rest simply with the announcement that "so is it written."

The key question that has to be faced is the problem of the foundation of obligation or duty. Why should a man ever do anything as an act of duty? To act in a particular way because it pleases us to do so, or because it seems to us that the act will lead to an end which we find desirable is reasonable enough. Any man can make sense out of that kind of behavior. But traditional morality demands far more of us. We are asked to do things which we are not inclined to do, which in fact we find difficult and contrary to our desires, and to refrain from doing things that strike us as temptingly attractive and pleasant. Such morality frequently requires us to behave in ways which run counter to our inclinations or to forego by a deliberate act of will that toward which we are inclined. Reflective men will quite properly question such moral rules. A classic statement of the problem is found in Plato's *Republic* where Glaucon challenges Socrates to defend his morality. Imagine, he says, that a man was in possession of the magical ring of Gyges which gives him the power to make himself invisible at will. This means that he could do anything that he chose without any fear of being caught or punished. Given this power, says Glaucon, "no man can be imagined to be of such an iron nature that he would stand fast in justice. No man would keep his hands off what was not his own when he could safely take what he liked out of the market, or to go into houses and lie with any one at his pleasure, or kill or release from prison whom he would, and in all respects be like a God among men."[3] The problem for moral philosophy is clear enough. Is there any reason, other than fear of punishment, why a man should feel himself bound by any rules of moral behavior? Translated into Jewish terms, one may ask whether the fear of punishment, human or divine, is the only motive for observing the commandments. In an age when even many traditional theologians are embarrassed by the sole reliance on divine punishment, it seems abundantly clear that a mature Jewish morality must seek to base itself on some other foundation.

One can imagine the thoughtful child in the Jewish school subjecting to proper and critical questioning even the most commonly accepted moral rules. Given the temper of our society, which of the Ten Commandments continues to be axiomatic in our day? Jewish education which does not choose to address itself to such questions is stubbornly blind. Jewish education which does not know how to address itself to such questions is tragically deficient. Here is one area, one of many, where serious philosophical scholarship can provide intellectual guidance for educators who are seeking a Jewishly authentic and intellectually honest and responsible approach to such questions. This may smack of apologetics, but I see no reason to reject, as improper, serious and sophisticated efforts to understand, and through such understanding to defend, traditional Jewish norms of moral behavior.

At the outset, it is necessary to establish the legitimacy and propriety of carrying on such inquiry in the context of Jewish education. Admittedly, there is a strain in classical Judaism that rejects all such inquiry as improper. For those who subscribe to this position the watchword is, *"Gezerah hi milefanai; en lekha reshut leharher ahareha."* [4] Whatever may be said in defense of this position, it is thoroughly anti-philosophical and anti-rational. One of the main tasks of Jewish philosophy is to legitimate the enterprise of rational inquiry. It is of the highest significance for Jewish educational practice that the major Jewish philosophers, almost without exception, made a point of stressing that the use of human reason to understand divine things and ultimate human concerns is not only permissible but obligatory. A typical instance is offered by Bahya ibn Pakuda who concludes his discussion of this matter by observing that, "It has thus been demonstrated by arguments drawn from Reason, Scripture and Tradition that it is our duty rationally to investigate every topic on which we can, by the exercise of our mental faculties, attain clearness." [5] Similar sentiments are expressed by Saadia, Judah Halevi, Maimonides and others, and in almost every case the philosopher presents decisive evidence out of the tradition itself. Given the fact that these philosophers, and others like them, have an acknowledged place within the normative Jewish tradition, their stance with respect to the propriety of rational inquiry may be accepted as an unquestionably legitimate Jewish option. For educational purposes, they provide us with insights into and understanding of Judaism which are indispensable in an age of intellectual openness. If we suppose, as I do, that we cannot and should not make Jewish teaching purely authoritarian, then a study and understanding of the work of the philosphers provides us with a way of approaching even the most sensitive Jewish issues with uncompromising critical intelligence. This is in itself of inestimable importance for Jewish education, without regard to the particular subject matter which may be studied. It should be clear that the purely authoritarian stance is only one among various options within Jewish tradition, and that the option of rational inquiry is at least as legitimate, if not more legitimate, as a way of coming to terms with Jewish doctrine and faith.

Saadia and the Problem of Morality

Let us now consider the methods by which some Jewish philosophers addressed themselves to the problem of the foundations of morality. From the time of the earliest medieval Jewish philosophers on we see the reliance on Scriptural or rabbinic authority replaced by efforts to come to terms with this question through rational reflection. Saadia Gaon introduced the idea of *mitzvot sikhliyyot,* commandments which derive from reason. These are, on the whole, the moral commandments, and are distinguished by him from the purely ritual commandments which pose a different problem. So confident is Saadia that the moral commandments are dictated by reason, that he summarily dismisses as unworthy of consideration anyone who propounds another view. A claimant to prophecy who says to us, "My Lord commands you to commit adultery and steal" should not even be asked for any evidence in support of his claim, "since what he called upon us to do is not sanctioned by either reason or tradition." A defender of such a false prophet could only take refuge in what Saadia considers the patently absurd theory that "the disapproval of lying and the approval of the truth were not prompted by reason but were the result of the commandments and prohibitions of Scripture, and the same was true for the rejection of murder, adultery, and stealing. When he had come to that, however, I felt that I needed no longer concern myself with him and that I had my fill of discussion with him."[6]

Clearly, this is still no more than a dogmatic statement on Saadia's part and can hardly serve to satisfy us that moral rules have their foundation in the dictates of reason. Both philosophical analysis and the educational situation demand more of us. On what does Saadia base his claim? And what does he mean by "reason" in this context? To be fully satisfying he would have to show us that moral rules are rationally demonstrable, and "reason" would then be equivalent to the power of demonstration. This is the sense in which current philosophical usage would understand any claim that a given proposition was rationally certain. It would have to be seen as a necessary proposition, one which reason knows to be necessary either immediately or else by way of demonstration. Yet, a careful study of Saadia's treatment of the rational commandments reveals no such claim, nor even such a conception of what it means to assert that a proposition is rational. Part of the work of scholarship is to become clear about this matter in the philosophy of Saadia, as well as in the thought of others who adopt his view that there are rational commandments. Without clarification we have only a dogmatic assertion, whose meaning is unclear and whose ground is hidden. At best, this could be presented to students as an instance of uncritical dogmatism, but not as a rational way of dealing with the problem of moral obligation.

While works on Jewish ethics regularly record Saadia's established distinction between rational and traditional commandments, they fail to investigate the matter further. This is not only the failure of scholarship, it is also a failure to make possible in a serious way the translation of scholarship into material that is useful for Jewish education. Careful study reveals the troubling fact that despite his repeated references to rational commandments, Saadia nowhere offers an argument or a demonstration of their presumed rationality. It turns out, instead, that, in this context, "rational" simply means, "useful." The so-called rational commandments are those that have, in his view, such obvious personal or social utility that no reasonable man could possibly question their desirability and, hence, their binding force. Because of God's grace these commandments, though rational, are also recorded by the prophets, "so that we might not be left to roam at large without guidance."[7] This is merely a concession to the fact that men can be stupid and should be protected from their stupidity. Saadia believes, however, that even without divine commandment we could discover the rationality of these prescriptions, and therefore, that they bind us, above all, because our reason makes them mandatory.

When we come to examine what it is that reason teaches us with respect to morality, we discover that Saadia offers nothing more than prudential arguments. Murder is evil because "if license were to prevail in this matter, men would cause each other to disappear." Fornication is forbidden "in order that men might not become like the beasts with the general result that no one would know his father." Theft is forbidden because, "if it were permitted, some men would rely on stealing the other's wealth, and they would neither till the soil nor engage in any other gainful occupation."[8] These are typical of the arguments that Saadia offers in defense of the claim that morals are ultimately rooted in reason. It is essential to get beyond the terminology which speaks of these commandments as "rational" to the substance of the exposition in order to realize that we have here nothing more than the simplest of prudential claims about the utility of the moral commandments.

There is no respect in which these arguments can be considered truly rational in any contemporary sense of the term. They are not logically necessary. Their contraries do not involve internal contradictions. They are neither intuitively certain, nor demonstrated by some appropriate course of argument. At best, they are recommendations which tell us that if we seek the ends that are specified, experience teaches us that these commandments are reliable means for achieving those ends. If this is all that Saadia understands by rational morality, then he clearly cannot bring about our unqualified assent to the moral law. We may agree with his prudential assessments, but we cannot, in the light of today's understanding of these matters, view his argument as rationally binding. It would be an interesting and useful work of scholarship to discover why Saadia considered these arguments to be rational. But for the purposes of the school curriculum it is enough to note the limitations of the arguments that he offers.[9] We have here one way to approach questions concerning the grounds of moral obligation. On this reading, duty turns out to be nothing more than the application of good prudential sense to practical human situations. If we adopt such a view, then we should be seeking to persuade our students that the moral law of the Torah commends itself to them because it is clearly in their own best interests as well as in the best interests of society as a whole. Saadia offers us no resources with which to show them, as we might have hoped, that the moral law is in any objective sense rationally necessary.

In the history of Jewish thought this Saadianic pattern repeats itself numerous times. What emerges is the view that all the commandments, not only the moral commandments, have reasons, otherwise God who commands would be arbitrary and capricious. Abraham ibn Ezra asserts that the Torah was given only to men with intelligence "and whoever has no intelligence has no Torah." (ad Ex. 20:1) What is established, at best, by such arguments is only that the commandments have reasons, i.e. that they serve some useful purpose, but not that they are rational in the sense of being rationally demonstrable. The matter is stated precisely by Nahmanides when he says that in every divine commandment there is "a reason and a useful purpose and some benefit to man" *(taam vetoelet vetikkun leadam)*. (ad Deut. 22:6) The distinction that must be carefully maintained is that between having a reason and being rational. Commandments that have no reasons at all would be wildly arbitrary. Those that claim to serve a useful purpose and, in this respect, to have reasons, may be called rational in the weak sense that they do not contravene reason and that they recommend themselves to men of experience and sound judgment. They are not, however, rational in the strong sense of being required by reason. The weak sense of rational is hardly sufficient to persuade skeptics that the commandments, even the moral commandments, are binding. They can always point out that this depends on each man's evaluation of the practical situation in which he finds himself, on the ends which he happens to value, and on the actual conditions which prevail at that particular time and place. Despite the extravagant statements of Saadia and those who followed in his path, it is not obvious that any man is bound either by reason or experience to acknowledge that the moral commandments are permanently binding even in the weak sense that they are always socially useful. The most casual acquaintance with the attitudes and practices of contemporary society provides sufficient evidence that many intelligent men categorically reject this claim in theory and in practice.

For the student, who is searching, and for the teacher, who must give guidance, this prudential approach to morality offers a possible but not a necessary direction. Reflection on the moral life in its various aspects may lead to the conclusion that this utilitarian conception is all that is open to us. It may also lead to the conclusion that this is a sound Jewish understanding of the basis of morality. It may, but it need not lead to these conclusions. Other possibilities must, therefore, be studied.

The moral purposes of Jewish education would be well served, then, if we move to a consideration of the very different views of Maimonides.[10] With clarity of understanding that would do credit to a philosopher of any age, Maimonides goes directly to the heart of the issue. Moral principles, he holds, have nothing whatsoever to do with truth or falsehood. They are not matters of the intellect at all, and are, therefore, in no way determined by reason. It is simply a mistake to hold that reason sets rules of right and wrong. He refers, in a familiar passage, to the great error of construing moral matters as rational in character. "The evils which the philosophers term such... are things which all people commonly agree are evils, such as the shedding of blood, theft, robbery, fraud, injury to one who has done no harm, ingratitude, contempt for parents, and the like.... Some of our later sages, who were infected with the unsound principles of the *Mutkallimun,* called these rational laws."[11] It is generally agreed that the reference to "our later sages" is directed at Saadia Gaon. In language which could have been written by a contemporary Anglo-American philospher, Maimonides argues that moral statements have no cognitive content. They assert nothing about the world. Neither are they purely analytic. It follows from this that they are not rational in character and cannot, in themselves, be either true or false.

This is a position so strong that, with the possible exception of Kant, I do not believe any philosopher has succeeded in defending its contrary. Many have spoken, like Saadia, about a rational morality. However, none have succeeded in offering us a persuasive account of the supposed rational foundations of the rules of moral behavior. Our work is to discover on what ground Maimonides believed that intelligent and thoughtful men could accept as binding the very morality whose rationality he denies in principle.

Maimonides and the Problem of Morality

Maimonides sees only two possible ways of approaching the problem of the foundations of morality. Either morality is nothing more than a set of social conventions, or else it is divine commandment. In the former case, it has no independent internal binding force whatsoever. Moral conventions are observed by reasonable men only because they recommend themselves as useful or attractive, or because they are enforced by social pressure or by the power of the sovereign. In a morality of social convention there is no answer to the challenge of Plato's Glaucon. Given the assurance of not being caught, there is no sensible reason why a man should not do whatever he finds attractive even if it violates convention or defies the will of the sovereign. This is, in fact, the condition in which Maimonides believes all secular moral theories leave us. But do not Saadia and his followers expose us to precisely the same danger, since they leave us finally, with nothing more stable than personal appraisals of what is to our advantage? The only viable alternative, according to Maimonides, is to accept the biblical doctrine that the commandments are divine in origin. Since

God is the one ultimately good and wise being, his commandments are not arbitrary, but are the most perfect way for man
to achieve his highest self-fulfillment.

The strategy of Maimonides is not to offer an argument,
but to pose alternatives. He rejects argument as inappropriate
because the subject-matter of ethics is not cognitive. To claim
to offer a rational defense of morality, in the strict sense of
"rational" is to be guilty of irredeemable intellectual confusion. Only when we are clear about the limits of our intellect
in its capacity to deal with moral issues, can we face our problem honestly and in the full awareness of the gravity of our
situation. If reason cannot solve our moral problems, then we
stand on the brink of sheer moral arbitrariness. It was the intense
desire to avoid this danger that led philosophers to seek fixed
objective rational foundations for morality. However, they
failed, as they inevitably had to fail, for, viewed philosoph-
ically, moral distinctions are, according to Maimonides, like
aesthetic distinctions, only a matter of taste. This being the case,
we must either acknowledge that the Sophists were right, and
that, at least with respect to morality, there is no fixed rule, but
man is the measure of all things. Or else, we must find some
other non-philosophical ground for morality. At this point,
Maimonides is able to fall back on the teachings of Jewish
tradition without the risk of being arbitrary or closeminded.
What he says is that, lacking rational foundations, we must seek
the very best alternative basis for our morality. Admittedly, he
offers us no more than an act of faith that affirms the true divinity of the scriptural text. He does so without pretense, and with
complete clarity. When he engages in the serious search for
viable moral options, he concludes that we either have no
morality or a divinely based morality. Given the price we are
forced to pay if we adopt the former alternative with its con-

comitant moral anarchy, it seems wise for faithful Jews to accept the latter as a necessary condition for the preservation not only of their Jewishness, but of their very humanity.

For purposes of Jewish education in the contemporary school this may seem to be a highly unsatisfactory position. How can an appeal to faith meet the relativistic skepticism of our society? What is required, I believe, is a more careful and subtle study of the issue. It can be shown readily enough that the foundation of morality, as we normally understand and practice it, is the conviction that man is a being of special worth. Such expressions as "the dignity of man," "the unalienable rights of men," "the preciousness of human personality" and similar ways of speaking, all point to this conviction. Without the distinction between man and all other creatures, there is no basis for our kind of morality. Why else give our accustomed priority to the value of human life? How else justify the use of all that is in the world for the needs and purposes of man? How else explain our right to eat living things (and plants are also living things) in order to sustain ourselves? How else account for our readiness to use animals in medical experiments that are aimed at alleviating human suffering? On what other ground can we justify our duties to respect other men, to be kind, compassionate, loving, even when it is not to our personal advantage? The denial of the distinction — the essential qualitative distinction — between men and all other creatures is the key step in the undermining of all morality as we understand it.

Other Philosophic Approaches to Morality

Philosophers have at various times tried to deny this special claim about human worth, and in doing so have also given up morality, as we understand it. Some have struggled to protect morality by preserving the claims of a special human dignity, even while rejecting the theoretical foundations on which such claims rest. Others have been satisfied to accept without protest the moral skepticism which is the result of their conviction that man is merely one more animal. The line stretches from antiquity to contemporaries like B.F. Skinner. Plutarch takes up the issue in his *Moralia*[13] when he treats the case of Gryllus, a man who has been transformed into a swine. Circe offers to change Gryllus back into a man if Odysseus can persuade him that men are truly superior to the beasts. Despite mighty efforts, Odysseus fails. Gryllus counters all his arguments by trying to show that, "The Soul of beasts has a greater natural capacity and perfection for the generation of virtue" than the souls of men. Moreover, he argues that animals "have a natural endowment of reason and intellect," so that there is no ground for claiming that men have any special worth. Similar views can be found throughout the history of western thought. In every case they present a profoundly serious challenge to traditional morality because they reject the foundations on which that morality rests.[14]

The challenge posed by this denial of the special worth and superiority of men cannot be met satisfactorily by mere counterassertion. It was attempted by John Stuart Mill, and his failure is evident to even the moderately perceptive student. Mill offers no argument in favor of the superiority of man, nor does he provide a metaphysical or theological structure which would account for this supposed superiority. Instead, in a frequently quoted passage, he merely proclaims that man is superior. "Few human creatures," he says, "would consent to be changed into any of the lower animals for a promise of the fulfillment of a beast's pleasures.... It is better to be a human being dissatisfied than a pig satisfied; better to be Socrates dissatisfied than a fool satisfied. And if the fool, or the pig, are of a different opinion, it is because they only know their own side of the question. The other party to the comparison knows both sides." The slightest reflection will show that this is clearly not an argument, nor does Mill provide any evidence for his claim. The fact is that "the other party to the comparison" does not know both sides. No man 'has ever been a pig literally, nor was Socrates ever a fool. If it is a matter merely of experience, then we have no basis whatsoever for our confidence that men are superior, for we have no direct knowledge of what it is to be an animal. Nothing that Mill has to say would have served to persuade Plutarch's Gryllus, nor can it stand as a serious counterweight to any doctrine which reduces man to the status of just one more animal.

Unhappily, even the most serious and sophisticated attempts to deal with the problem in purely philosophical fashion have not succeeded. The best example is to be found in Kant's ethical writings. Out of the elaborate reflections on which he bases his moral philosophy Kant emerges with the principle that man is of such supreme worth that he alone must always be treated as an end in himself, never merely as a means. Students of Kant have found it extremely difficult to find any justification for this claim that man has unique intrinsic worth. A detailed examination of the issue as it unfolds in Kant is beyond the scope of this paper. What is essential for our purpose is the recognition that major philosophers have seen that morality rests on affirming the special value of man, and that they have struggled mightily, but with little success, to justify their claims about human dignity and value.

Jewish tradition has its own way of dealing with the problem. Man is conceived from the very beginning as a special being created in the image of God, and it is by virtue of that fact alone that he has special status and special value. It is this

which gives ground to and makes sense out of the whole range
of moral rules and prescriptions which are aimed at preserving
the dignity and holiness of human beings as such. In this
tradition man is understood as rising to his own proper human
fulfillment only by way of *imitatio dei*. "You shall be holy
for I the Lord your God am holy." Maimonides recognizes the
full force of this tradition and sees that it alone can provide
an adequate foundation for morality. I take it to be not without
significance that the first chapter of the *Guide of the Perplexed*
deals with the interpretation of the terms *tselem* and *demut*,
image and likeness, and that the very first verse which it quotes
and interprets is the verse, "Let us make man in our image,
after our likeness." Equally significant for our purpose is the fact
that his second chapter deals with the problem of the foundations of moral principles, and that Maimonides ends it with a
verse from Psalms, "Adam, unable to dwell in dignity, is like
the beasts that speak not."[16] Careful study should convince the
perceptive reader that Maimonides is here addressing himself
to the problem of the ground of morality. He is affirming that
without the recognition that man is a special being created in the
divine image there can be no morality. He also affirms that
morality is dependent on divine commandments, but that these
can only be addressed to this one special being who has in his
nature a divine element. His position depends on a very carefully worked out doctrine about the nature of man and the nature
of God. There is here no arbitrariness, but rather a closely
developed metaphysic and a sophisticated philosophical anthro-
pology. These reflections gain their particular importance when
they are joined to the sheer logical point that moral distin-
tions in themselves have no truth-value. Once all these pieces
have been set out, we have a doctrine which gives serious
grounding to morality, while fully recognizing the limits of what

can be known. Within these limits, however, Maimonides offers us more than a mere dogmatic affirmation. Rather, he helps us see that since man alone has the power of reason, only he can be understood as a creature in the image of God. This power distinguishes him from all other creatures and gives him special status and value, but does not itself specify how that value is to be served and that status recognized in practice. Reason confers value, but, contrary to Kant it does not have the power to legislate morality. Here we face the choice of either risking the degradation, even the destruction, of man, or accepting the validity and the binding force of the divine moral imperatives. Maimonides makes what seems to him the only wise choice, namely, as a Jew to accept the moral teaching of the tradition and, in that way, to preserve the preciousness of man. In any school discussion of the foundations·of morality this essentially religious move provides an important alternative. Students can be helped to see that even the most rigorously rational thinker must sometimes go beyond the limits of what pure reason authorizes and authenticates. He does so when what hangs in the balance is of such crucial importance to man and society that the risk of transcending the limits of reason seems to be fully justified. This is precisely what Maimonides did.

Buber's Moral Concern

It will help illuminate the discussion further if we give some consideration to the way in which a contemporary Jewish thinker has approached the problem of the foundations of morality. Martin Buber differs profoundly in his style of thought and in his personal religious commitments from the medieval Jewish philosophers with whom we have been dealing. Yet he is similar to them in his passionate moral concern, and in his conviction that the grounds or morality must be carefully explored.

The differences are easy to set forth. Unlike Saadia, Buber categorically rejects all utilitarian conceptions of morality. He understands by "the ethical in the strict sense the yes and no which man gives to the conduct and actions possible to him, the radical distinction between them which affirms or denies them not according to their usefulness or harmfulness for individuals and society, but according to their intrinsic value and disvalue." [17] Buber consistently maintains this pure anti-utilitarian position. Whatever it is that grounds moral values, it is never, in his view, the mere fact that they happen to serve man's needs or interests.

Unlike Maimonides, Buber denies that we have any direct knowledge of divine moral commandments. He takes very seriously indeed, divine revelation, but it is never, in his view, a revelation of specific rules or prescriptions. This point is made explicit by him many times. He writes, for example, that, "God has truth, but He does not have a system. He expresses this truth through his will, but his will is not a program." [18] Or again, "I do not believe that revelation is ever a formulation of a law." [19] And, in perhaps the most familiar of all his statements on the subject, "For me, though man is a law-receiver, God is not a law-giver, and therefore the Law has no universal validity for me, but only a personal one. I accept, therefore, only what I think is being spoken to me...." [20]

Nevertheless, Buber considers moral values to be absolute. A Jew will not find them simply dictated in the Torah, but neither are they invented. In discussing this subject elsewhere,[21] I expressed Buber's view in the following way. "Every moral decision (as distinct from prudential choice) presumes the absoluteness of the claim which is made on us, the absoluteness of our duty. This absoluteness does not derive from ourselves. It is not a feeling within us. It is an ontological reality which we discover when we allow ourselves to face our duty and to hear that which is addressed to us. I am constitutionally incapable,' says Buber, 'of conceiving of myself as the ultimate source of moral approval or disapproval of myself, as surety for the absoluteness that I to be sure, do not possess, but nevertheless imply with respect to this yes or no. The encounter with the original voice, the original source of yes or no, cannot be replaced by any self-encounter.' ''[22] Buber appears to be saying that when a man confronts moral issues with his full being he will discover in the moral situation what his duty is. This duty is, somehow, given, but never as direct divine commandment, never as a fixed law or permanently binding rules.

While rejecting traditional views concerning revelation, and denying the Maimonides position that the moral law can only be either divine revelation or pure social convention, Buber still wants to retain the absoluteness and the objectivity of moral values. His technique is to substitute a kind of phenomenology of the moral life for older doctrines of revelation. In effect, he is saying that any serious examination of genuine moral experience will confirm his thesis that man does not invent, but discovers moral values, and that he discovers them in such way that he knows himself to be absolutely bound by them. We have here a strikingly different philosophic stance, one in which phenomenological analysis of the moral experience takes the place of rational analysis of moral concepts. He appears to agree with Maimonides that reason alone cannot legislate morality, but unlike Maimonides, he is convinced that there are objective moral values which man discovers directly in experience. So firm is his confidence in his position that he considers any attack on it a kind of madness.

When, in a paper on Buber's moral philosophy, I raised a question concerning the seeming privacy of moral judgment

and its attendant dangers, Buber refused even to discuss the
issue. To me it seemed clear that once we say that a man must
find the answers to moral questions within himself, we always
risk confrontation with those who deviate from our moral norms
and justify themselves by saying that they know in all certainty
that this is what is demanded of them. "What shall we do,"
I asked, "with the man who chooses a way in opposition to the
norms of our society or to the Ten Commandments? Shall we
condemn him as evil? But we cannot for he may be acting in
accordance with what he is convinced is the voice of God."[23]
To this Buber replied in the following way. "Now, however,
Fox strides to the decisive blow. But what then shall we do,
he asks, with the criminal who — I must cite it literally — 'May
be acting in accordance with what he is convinced is the voice
of God?' Must I explicitly state that this hypothetical instance
is absurd, for then it would be a madman that one was talking
of, who indeed might hold himself to be God? A man who
is not mad can only believe that he is following the voice of God
if he acts with his whole soul... As I say ever again, however,
one cannot do evil with the whole soul... ." It seems to me
clear that there is here no answer to the challenge for Buber
is saying only that whoever acts in a way radically opposed
to what he (Buber) sees as good can only be either mad or evil.
Yet, why should Buber's private insights be normative for all
men?

My purpose is not to engage in a polemic against Buber,
but rather to illustrate a point. So strong is the impulse, or the
need, to retain the absoluteness of moral values, that Buber was
unable even to conceive that there could be a serious challenge
to his position. It would teach a good deal to our students about
the inner drive toward morality if they were to confront the case
of Buber. It might help them to realize again how much is at stake

in rejection of the traditional moral norms, so much, in fact, that profoundly intelligent men who can produce no theory to sustain their moral absolutes are still unable to give them up.

This point is even more clearly evident in the case of Buber if we take note of a striking paradox. Though he explicitly denies, over and over, that there can ever be fixed moral rules laid down in advance and permanently binding, Buber does himself frequently affirm such rules. He holds, for example, that lying is evil; that violence is evil; that murder is evil; that the drive for power is evil. He makes similar pronouncements about what is good. If students would note this remarkable fact, they would be helped considerably in their own moral reflections. Buber is, after all, a man of the highest intelligence. If he is guilty of what appear to be gross internal contradictions, it is not simply the result of inattention or oversight. It must stem from the fact that, despite his theory, he cannot give up the very law whose existence he denies. He cannot give up because he recognizes fully (despite his professed anti-utilitarianism) the monstrous consequences for individuals and for society. For him, man is unique in that he "is the being who is capable of becoming guilty and is capable of illuminating his guilt."[25] It is, according to Buber, the capacity to be moral, to know and to abide by moral values, that distinguishes man and defines his humanity. With this view of man's nature, joined to his own personal sense of the nature of moral experience, Buber is able to sustain, to his own satisfaction, his belief in objective moral values. At the same time, because he wants to preserve the autonomy of the moral agent, he is moved to deny that there is a fixed moral law. Students would do well indeed to confront such a case, and to realize that profoundly serious and intelligent men often find it necessary to live and cope with inescapable inner dialectical tensions. Both life and thought, in such a case, would appear to rise above simple logic. Perhaps it is because, as Bergson thought, logic is a tool with which man is able to manipulate things in the world, but not the instrument by which man discovers and expresses what is essential to his own humanity, much less his divinity.

In these treatments of the problem of morality we have a classic case of the way in which scholarship is relevant to the work of lower-level education. No Jewish education can ignore the challenge of moral instruction. Neither can any serious Jewish education ignore the challenges to Jewish morality posed by contemporary society. Even the youngest student can be helped to see the various ways in which Jewish thinkers have tried to come to terms with these problems. They can be shown that their own concerns were, in certain respects, shared by the greatest minds that Jewish learning produced. They will discover that Judaism does not expect blind and unthinking acceptance of its dogmas. They will see that inquiry, reflection, critical analysis are not only permitted but expected. In the process of study they will also come to realize that there are no easy answers to very complex questions. Finally, it will be evident that, having pushed rational reflection to its farthest limits, we are forced to take our stand with less than absolute certainty. It will be important for them to understand how much is at stake in such decision, to know what price we pay for the stance we take, what risks we run, what we sacrifice and what we gain. The fact that Jewish thinkers of very diverse tempers and styles of thought chose to remain committed to the observance of the commandments ought to evoke the interest of students. They must come to see why, despite their differences, both Saadia and Maimonides continue to cherish and observe the law. What are the values which, even when not fully defended, are yet so important that Jews cannot yield them?

How shall we understand the fact that later thinkers, e.g. Buber, who rejected the ritual commandments, continue, nevertheless, to be fully committed to the moral law? In translating sophisticated scholarship into the answers to questions of this order we shall be creating the bridge between the world of high learning and the world of the student. Without that bridge the student's world will be irredeemably narrow and constricted. With it he begins his true education.

NOTES

1. This paper is based, in part, on some of my own published work which deals with the themes that are discussed. I believe that, despite the seeming immodesty, this offers a good opportunity to confront in a concrete instance the problem of the relationship of serious scholarly work to educational practice. The specific references will be given at the appropriate places.

2. It would be of great value and interest to examine the ways in which the rabbinic tradition deals with the theoretical foundations of morality, but that topic is beyond the limits of this study.

3. Plato, *Republic,* 560 bc.

4. Cf., *Yoma* 67b; Rashi, ad Numbers, 19:2; and others in the rabbinic literature which make the same point with minor variations.

5. *Hovot Halevavot, Shaar Hayihud,* Ch. 3.

6. Saadia Gaon, *The Book of Beliefs and Opinions,* III, 8; Rosenblatt edition, p. 164.

7. *Ibid.,* III, 1, p. 138. Saadia also holds that we need revelation to teach us in detail how to carry out the general prescriptions of the rational commandments; *cf., ibid.,* III, 3.

8. *Ibid.,* III, 2, p. 141.

9. This discussion of Saadia is based, in part, on a paper on the problem of rational commandments in Saadia given at the World Congress of Jewish Studies, August 1973. In it I seek to develop fully the analysis of the text and the key terms, as well as the historical antecedent of Saadia's position. The paper will appear in the *Proceedings* of the Congress and in *Jewish Ethics in Theory and Practice,* edited by Marvin Fox (Ohio State University Press, 1974).

10. For an extended discussion of this topic, cf., Marvin Fox, "Maimonides Aquinas on Natural Law," *Diné Israel,* (Tel-Aviv University Faculty of Law), Vol. III, 1972, pp. V-XXXVI.

11. Joseph I. Gorfinkel (tr. & ed.), *The Eight Chapters of Maimonides on Ethics,* (New York, 1912), pp. 76-77.

12. It is well-known that Maimonides devotes much energy to discovering reasons for the commandments. However, it would be a mistake to suppose that he considers these reasons sufficient in themselves, so that we could dispense with divine commandment. He understands fully the distinction between having a reason and being rationally necessary. He also understands that prudential considerations, in themselves, cannot be morally decisive. It is only if these prudential considerations are seen as divinely ordained that we can acknowledge them as fully binding, for in that case we are invoking perfect divine wisdom, not fallible human judgment.

13. In the section, "Beasts are Rational."

14. For an extended discussion of this topic, cf., Marvin Fox, "Religion and Human Nature in the Philosophy of David Hume," in *Process and Divinity: The Hartshorne Festschrift,* Wm. R. Reese and Eugene Freeman, eds., (Open Court, 1964), pp. 561-577.

15. John Stuart Mill, *Utilitarianism,* (New York, 1948), Ch. II, pp. 9-10.

16. Psalms 49:13, as rendered by S. Pines in his translation of *The Guide of the Perplexed.* This translation of an admittedly difficult and disputed verse reflects accurately Maimonides' understanding of it in the context of his discussion.

17. Martin Buber, *Eclipse of God,* (New York, 1957), p. 95.

18. Martin Buber, *Israel and the World,* (New York, 1948), p. 114.

19. Letter to Franz Rosenzweig, June 24, 1924. Cited in Franz Rosenzweig, *On Jewish Learning,* (New York, 1955), p. 111.

20. *Ibid.,* p. 115.

21. For a full discussion of some of the relevant issues cf., Marvin Fox, "Some Problems in Buber's Moral Philosophy," in *The Philosophy of Martin Buber,* Paul A. Schilpp and Maurice Friedman (eds.), pp. 151-170. See also in that volume, Buber's "Reply," pp. 698-700; 718-721. I have

chosen to base my discussion of Buber largely on these sources since they offer a very clear instance of the way in which scholarly work and scholarly controversy illuminate the issues with which we are concerned in this paper. Moreover, since Buber disavowed so vigorously the views which I attribute to him, it is only fair to the reader to call to his attention Buber's own statement on the subject.

22. Fox, op. cit., p. 153.

23. *Ibid.*, p. 162.

24. Buber, "Reply," *op. cit.,* p. 720. It would help students also to learn to pay attention to seemingly small details. Where I spoke of a "man," Buber turns him into a "criminal," thereby transforming the framework of the discussion and weighting it in a most serious way.

25. Martin Buber, *The Knowledge of Man,* (New York, 1965), p. 146.

4

JEWISH SCHOLARSHIP AND THE JEWISH COMMUNITY
A Reform Perspective

Alexander Schindler

I begin with a *hineni he-'ani mi-ma'as,*[1] an admission that I really have no place in such company. When Gerson Cohen graciously invited me to participate in this colloquium I assumed that my audience would be made up of laymen with a particular interest in Jewish education, religious school teachers, perhaps colleagues, and so I replied affirmatively. Imagine my embarrassment when some weeks later I received a partial listing of colloquium participants and read there the names of men who have a lifetime of experience in a field in which I was scarcely tested, among them also scholars of the first rank who have taught me so much. They should not be asked to listen to me. I should be content to be in their place, listening to them, learning from them. I am certainly not a scholar; my four years as the Director of Education of the Union of American Hebrew Congregations barely qualify me to be called an educator. I suppose that as the leader of a national congregational body I represent not the academy, nor the school, but rather the community; I am the spokesman for its claims.

In attempting to determine the exact nature of my assignment. I conferred with the organizer of the conference and we finally concluded that my contribution would be to respond to the scholars assembled here, to attack the core of the problem. Is there indeed a gap between high-level scholarship and the classroom? In what ways can it be bridged?

My topic, therefore, is *Jewish Scholarship and the Jewish Community* with the sub-title, *A Reform Perspective*. Not because I am particularly parochial in my concerns, but because the world bounded by Reform Jewish students is that world which is familiar to me. When I speak of Jewish education, therefore, I have in mind the practices of Reform religious schools and the theory and curriculum evolved by Reform Judaism's Commission on Religious Education. And when I refer to Jewish scholars, I think primarily of those who teach in our seminary, or those who teach at various universities throughout the land, who are graduates of our schools and are still in one way or another identified with us. Any resemblance to other Jewish scholars living or dead is strictly coincidental.

I begin with the assumption that the linkage between the academy and the classroom, between higher-level Jewish scholarship and elementary or secondary Jewish education, is something more than a desideratum, that it is an essential ingredient of our community's continuity. Jewish students deserve that knowledge which flows from the Jewish scholar's thought and work. Those educational resources which we provide them ought to reflect it. And the Jewish scholar, in turn, should offer it, and not just indirectly through the insight which is implicit in his work, but rather explicitly so and in direct response to his understanding of the students' needs and of those identity problems with which they grapple.

It is a linkage which existed in the past, at least according to my intuitive perception. Perhaps I gild the past with a glitter which it does not deserve, but I believe it was so especially during those periods in our history when our community was

more or less closed. The scholar was something more than a
guardian of past treasures; he was a part of the community; he
lived in it; often he was its designated head. And the student,
wonders to relate, actually saw him in the flesh, saw him therefore not just as the imparter of knowledge but also as an
exemplar of those values which that knowledge enshrines. There
was a flow, from scholar to student to community and back
again.

This flow, whatever its force may have been at various
times, has certainly slowed in our time. There is a lag of considerable length between what is thought in our academies and
what is taught in our schools. Franz Rosenzweig, alluding to
the tradition of the "academic quarter hour," that time period
during which German university students were compelled to
wait for their docent, spoke of an "academic quarter century,"
which separates Jewish scholarship and the Jewish community.
This lag is due not only to the sheer physical distance which
sets us all apart, not only to the openness of our society, to
our increasing mobility and the fragmentation which ensues,
nor is it due only to an insufficiency of communication between
scholar and educator, nor even to the obtuseness of the student
or his unwillingness to learn. It is due also, and in no small
measure, to a disjoining of tasks, a sundering of that unity
of purpose which once bound Jewish scholarship and the Jewish
school. Today the scholar pursues his quest for truth, and the
teacher wants to help the student come to terms with his Jewishness. Viewed from such a perspective, the time lag may well
be in the reverse: sometimes and in certain respects Jewish
scholarship trails the Jewish community by a number of years.

In fact, there is such a two-fold lag today. The teachers
of Jewish studies in our seminaries and on campus have the
right to complain, and they do, that those students emerging

from Jewish schools are mostly ill-prepared, that most of them learned too little, and that so much of what they learned falls far below the level of understanding which contemporary Jewish scholarship has reached. They were taught a kind of pre-Newtonian Judaism in a post-Einsteinian age. Yet the teachers of these schools, and especially those who are charged with evolving the curriculum and preparing its supportive materials, have an equally valid counter-plaint: that in their effort to help the student in his becoming Jewish — which involves not just the transmission of knowledge, but also the energizing of the will to be Jewish and an enablement to express that will, to translate it from *midrash* to *maaseh* in the modern world — that in these larger efforts the fruitage of modern Jewish scholarship does not serve sufficiently. Our Jewish college students re-echo these sentiments, and on both counts. They tell us that we taught them too little, that we did not really challenge their intellect, that we mistook emotion for insight, that we gave them not much more than a child's notion of Judaism. But they also tell us that those Judaica courses which they take on campus (or at the seminaries, for that matter) and the books which are available to them for study only scarcely consider those questions which perplex them as they seek to be Jews and act as Jews in the modern world.

Are the students correct in their critique? And how much are scholars and academicians to blame?

The professionalization of Jewish scholarship is the first and foremost reason for this denial of the community's claim on its scholars. Many, most reform Jewish scholars simply do not see it their function to respond to it. They see themselves as professional scholars, citizens of the academic world, fully loyal to its canons of objectivity and value-free research. A deepening of the student's Jewish commitment might be a by-product but is not a design of their doing. A colleague of mine, who occupies a chair in biblical literature in a Midwestern university put the matter bluntly: "I am not a functionary of the Jewish community," he said, "I approach my teaching as I do my research, with objectivity and dispassion. It is my task neither to defend, nor to criticize, but to illuminate. It certainly isn't my job to resolve issues of faith or to coddle students who have problems with their Jewish identity. We have Hillel directors and Jewish chaplains for that." My friend's tongue is sharper than his teeth. He has helped many a student with such problems. He is presently engaged in co-authoring a text for our religious schools. He is a committed Jew. So are many, most Jewish scholars. Their very choice of profession gives evidence of at least antecedent convictions. But when they give expression to these convictions by devoting a portion of their work to these concerns or by becoming personally involved in the community or school, they tend to see these expressions as something apart from their work, totally alien to its higher purposes. And there's the rub.

Oddly enough, a not dissimilar attitude predominated at Hebrew Union College. At least it did in my day, and that was not so long ago. Of course, issues of belief were raised, but only in a scant handful of courses. Other subjects were approached with strict, almost exclusively academic bent. Bible was the place for text analysis; we never really got to see the whole. In history, economic factors consumed our concern; they were seen as the sole force in determining the course of Israel's wanderings. And in Hebrew, language skill was the goal; words were translated literally, their wider context was not explored; and all those rules about the *dagesh hazak*[2] did not serve to make us conscious of the *pintele Yid.*[3] In a word, everything was kept as free as possible from the taint of *odium theologicum.* I exaggerate to make a point (forgive an occasional lapse into hyperbole; it is a rabbinic weakness) but the point has its truth: even at a rabbinic school we find frequent and radical divergence between the intent of the scholar-teacher and the need of the student. In all fairness, I should add that we perceive the stirrings of a newer spirit in Cincinnati, that the school and its scholars must direct the student, not just in his quest for knowledge, but for meaning, too. It is interesting to remember, in this connection, that the *Wissenschaft des Judentums,* [4] which began that process of professionalization leading to scholarship's abandonment of the identity needs of the community, was itself, paradoxically, a response to a need of that community which spawned it. Zunz's call for the scientific study of Judaism and its literary heritage was not motivated merely by the desire to preserve these, but also by the hope that the scholarly endeavors would lead to a greater appreciation of Judaism and to the more ready acceptance of the Jew. The needs of the community moved him as much as did his concern for its literary heritage. But the spiritual descendants of Zunz see only one purpose for their work: to preserve that heritage of learning and to expand it.

Another factor which slows the flow from the academy to the school and back again is the academy's preoccupation with the past. Modern-day Jewish scholarship is still in the main past-oriented. That's what Jewish learning was all about from its beginnings, I suppose; conviction compelled rabbinic scholars to refer, and always to defer, to the Torah. *Die Wissenschaft* did not really redirect this orientation; it opted for new, more modern methods; but the goal, as we have seen, was to preserve what the past had to offer and so the focus remained and still is on the past. The past is glorified, the present neglected, the future all but ignored.

Contemporary Jewish studies are still not given their proper place in the constellation of scholarly creativity. Of course, there are those who labor devotedly in this field, but think of the imbalance — they are the few against the many. The preposition against is not ill-chosen, for one can sense almost an antagonism here, by those who constitute the establishment in Jewish academia. It is the classicist's disdain for the social sciences, born of a presumption that the present is brutish and that only the past is worthy of serious study. This disfavor — it must be noted at this Melton gathering — is bestowed with special intensity on the work of education. Its chairs in our seminaries are not most coveted or honored, and not because the men who fill or filled them are not deserving of honor; it is their concern which is held in scant regard, pious avowals of the importance of Jewish education to the contrary notwithstanding. The rabbinic student senses this disdain, internalizes it, and after ordination turns his back on the school.

In our schools the study of the past likewise still predominates. Efforts have been made of late to alter the approach to teaching, to make it thematic rather than historical, systematic rather than developmental. But by and large these efforts have been feeble in their effect. How could it be otherwise, since so much of the needed supportive scholarly work is lacking? The educator can well be asked to keep abreast of the scholar. He cannot be expected to lead him. We do not argue that the study of the past should be neglected, or that it should be subordinated to the study of the present. We argue for greater balance.

One more matter must be brought to light in this context. I refer to the historicism which has come to characterize much of Reform Jewish scholarship and whose fundamental assumptions are scarcely if ever questioned by that scholarship. Historicism leads to relativism which culminates in nihilism; it is not compatible with any concept of transcendence. Thus, when we apply the methods of historical research to the corpus of Jewish literature and thought and then see it in all its patterned divergence — ideas appearing from many sources blending with one another then disappearing again, all without a metabolizing principle independently rooted either in nature or beyond, for history sees only Jews as agents of this blending — such a view inevitably prompts the question whether there is after all a Jewish idea, never mind a Jewish point of view. There is a need, then, carefully to probe those assumptions on which so much of modern scholarship is based.

Which brings us directly to another node in that network of causes contributing to that lag problem with which we are concerned: the disinclination of most of our scholars to deal with questions of value. The professional factor undoubtedly fosters this reluctance; there is the ever-present danger of crossing that line which separates the scholar from the apologist. Positivism clearly comes into play, with its insistence that facts and values are absolutely heterogeneous. Whatever the reason, an ethical neutrality obtains, which might be good and proper, were it not so rigid that not only moral judgment, but moral issues as well, are frequently disdained.

Few Reform Jewish scholars in their work address themselves to normative ethical issues. What little there is, is of the neighborhood variety, scarcely present-, never future-oriented. Nowhere, for instance, can we find a critical analysis, from a Jewish perspective, of some of those moral problems which biology's imminent mastery of genetic engineering is pressing on us. The philosophical enterprise in its entirety is shunned among us. Too few Reform Jewish scholars are concerned with the study of philosophy. And yet, no other study is of greater potential usefulness to Jewish education, since the history of

philosophy is the history of Judaism's response to outer intellectual challenge. I was amazed to see four people here who
have made this their field of concentration.

I do not suggest that Jewish scholarship is value-*rein*.
Values are after all an intrinsic element of that raw material
with which every Jewish scholar works. He may not evaluate
them, but he does not ignore them, he elucidates them by tracing
them to their origins, their causes, and so they are there, implicit
in the work. But the need of Jewish education demands that
they be made explicit and that they be related to the problem
of the present — much in the manner of that superb paper which
Marvin Fox placed before us. Jewish educators need more of
this, much more, from every scholar in every discipline.

Education, if it is to be successful, and this has long been
a pedagogical truism, must move from the more immediate
concerns of the student toward that material which the educator
wishes to transmit. Well, our students are not interested in facts
as much as values; moral issues are at the core of their concern. Begin with the facts in the teaching of the Holocaust —
the causes of German anti-Semitism, its evolution from dis-
crimination to extermination, the meaning of the Nuremberg
laws, of the concept of racial superiority, and so on — and
they will listen with half an ear. To reach them, we are better
advised to make some other matters a point of departure, moral
matters, issues whose resolution can help them in their quest
for faith, and for a life reflective of it. How does the Jew confront evil? How should we resist an enemy? Does collective
guilt obviate individual responsibility? What can we say about
the face of man after Auschwitz? And what about the face of
God: can we believe in Him in spite of it? These are the questions
that stir them. They cannot be avoided. Some effort must be
made to speak to them. And in his quest for an answer, the

teacher should be aided, not abandoned, by Jewish scholarship.

Now a word about one other problem with which Jewish scholarship confronts the school: its fragmentation, a splintering of the whole, the atomization of the totality of Jewish learning into tiny bits and pieces which, in their fractional state, cannot even begin to convey the greatness of the whole. This fragmentation is dramatized at the universities where Jewish subject matter is cut, and then kept segregated, to fit the mold of the ivy-covered rubrics. But the process of education, if it is to be successful, requires a *gestalt*, a unity of form and matter.

Within the various disciplines, there is a like fragmentation. Jewish scholars, not unlike other scholars, have a hesitancy to generalize; they like to wait until all the facts are in. This hesitancy hinders the educative process, for the modern science of education has taught us that knowledge is best transmitted by means of organizing principles, and the more embracing they are the better. In recent Reform Jewish scholarship, Ellis Rivkin — agree with him or not — has been most daring in this respect.

The school has one more need of the scholar: that he enrich its work with his skills, not just by offering the disembodied yield of his learning, but by involving himself in its affairs. This grasp exceeds the scope of the scholar's professional responsibilities; it may even compete with them in that it steals that time and energy required for the proper pursuit of learning. But the professionalization of his calling has not yet obliterated the qualifying adjective "Jewish" — he is a student of Jewish lore, the guardian of the Jewish letters — and this Jewishness too has a valid claim on him. In a sense, the fulfillment of his professional purposes depends in no small measure on his response to this wider claim. For without that response — without the collective response of many scholars — the school and with it the community will sink into nothingness, and with it will go all the schools of higher learning and all the seminaries and all the chairs of Judaica on the American Jewish scene.

As for those who fear that this concern with problems of the Jewish community and an involvement in its work somehow perverts the nature of Jewish scholarship, let them not fear. And let them not be dismayed. Without this concern, modern Jewish scholarship would be neither modern nor Jewish.

NOTES

1. The first three words of a prayer recited by the *hazzan* during the High Holy Days Service, in which the supplicant speaks of his unworthiness for his task.

2. A grammatical term.

3. The quintessential Jew.

4. An intellectual movement of the early nineteenth century in Germany which emphasized the scientific study of Judaism.

5

THE CURRICULAR DELIBERATION

Ralph Tyler

The presentation by Professor Schwab and the conference discussions have emphasized the different perspectives provided by the several commonplaces in curriculum deliberations. However, I believe that we make a mistake if we view each individual participant as having only a single role to play in the deliberation process. It is entirely conceivable that, in a given situation, one person may play two or more roles. As I look around this room, I see scholars who are also dedicated teachers. But our teaching experience has not been with groups of children. If we were to be deliberating about what should be taught to 12-year-old children, for example, each of us would need to distinguish his areas of special competence, so that appropriate weight could be given to the merit of each suggestion. As a university scholar in the field of history, one's comments on matters of history will be given greater weight than suggestions about what 12-year olds can learn from history. On the other hand, as an experienced college teacher and as a scholar, one may speak with some weight about the intellectual skills of college students as well as about major conceptions of history.

A participant in curriculum deliberations should not be

inhibited by the notion that he has only one kind of contribution to make, as long as he recognizes the basis in study or experience that justifies the views he expresses.

Curriculum deliberations need not be and should not be limited to comments made only on matters on which the speaker is a recognized authority. Take my own case as an example. I would not know what to do if I were the teacher of a group of seven-year-olds. I have some ideas of what to do with a group of high school students because I've had experience with them. I spend a great deal of time, besides working on my field of scholarship, dealing with the problem of how to translate the insights of scholarship into forms useful for effective teaching of young people, ages 18 to 24. This means that I am not really divorced from scholarly activities nor from the problems of teaching and learning. I may be incompetent on certain matters lying within these fields, particularly when discussing an age group with whom I have had little experience, but I am not willing to renounce my concern for teaching problems. I am not disinterested and I am not wholly an amateur in the teaching field. When I participate in curriculum deliberations I speak to the points on which I have suggestions, but the weight of my comments must be judged in terms of the basis from which they are derived.

Another matter on which there may be confusion is the multiplicity of possible contributions a field of scholarship can make in education. Scholarship is almost infinite in its possibilities. Take history, for example. There is no limit to the number of things that Gerson Cohen or Ismar Schorsch could choose to study and to write about in depicting the history of the Jews, in general, or about a specific Jewish community. As scholars, the questions each one has to answer are: On what do I wish to focus my study? Am I interested in demography, in chronology, in institutional development, in intellectual movements, or what? The same question is faced in literature, philosophy, art, and other fields. One of the key elements in any scholarly enterprise is the focus of the scholar's study.

This has been recognized in the composition of this conference. Not every scholar on every faculty was invited to participate. Who were invited? As I look around this room, I believe the answer is: Scholars were invited who combine interest in their scholarship with interest in education, and whose special foci in their scholarly fields lend themselves to the translation process which Professor Schwab has outlined.

We are not saying at this conference: "Now you tell us the truth, and we shall translate it into the language of the classroom." The truth is infinite. Instead, we are saying, "We know that you are people who have the kinds of intellectual interest and concern that are likely to be significant in the context of the American Jewish situation and, particularly, the American Jewish classroom; now help us to adapt the interests and concerns you have to ones that are most meaningful in the education of children and youth."

In making these adaptations, the other commonplaces, in addition to the scholar, must be considered. Children are not meekly waiting to be told something by teachers and then faithfully trying to assimilate what they have been told. Children are usually active, directed by purposes which they have in mind, by habits, or by efforts to relieve discomfort. If a child is to give serious attention to schoolwork, what he is being taught must become part of his ongoing life. The understanding of the child in this sense must be provided among the commonplaces, partly by the teacher, partly by the parent, partly by the psychologist and, when possible, partly by the child.

It is a common assumption of those who develop the

curriculum that the school will help the child develop understanding, skills, attitudes, interests, and the like, and these
acquirements are to be employed by the child in the situations
he encounters where they are helpful. This transfer of training
from the classroom to life outside the school does not take place
automatically. The learner needs to perceive the relevance of
what he is learning to the out-of-school situations where it can
be helpfully employed, and often needs opportunities for guided
practice in using what he has learned. This understanding of
the child's milieu, his larger environment, should be furnished in
curriculum deliberations by the commonplaces of home and
community, represented in many cases by parent and sociologist,
but not necessarily restricted to them.

Some of the significant characteristics of children's learning
are not widely understood by those who develop curriculum
materials. For example, some may not realize that when a child
is confronted with something relatively complex, like a biblical
text, he quickly scans it, searching for something that appeals
to his interest and/or something that has meaning to him. If
he finds something that is interesting to him and/or has meaning,
he gives it further attention, seeking to comprehend it more fully
and to incorporate it into his "cognitive map," that is, his
interpretation of that part of his world in which he sees the
connection of the new material.

This characteristic of human learning has to be considered
when developing curriculum materials. For any material that
is complex, different children will find different aspects to
which they react and will learn different things from the
experience, as with the blind man's perception of the elephant.
This fact carries several implications. If the text is to stimulate
thinking about a particular matter, the teacher will need to call
the children's attention to that aspect of the text. He cannot

assume that all children will perceive this. If the text is to furnish experience in critical reading and interpretation, the teacher will need to help children with different interests and different levels of reading find appropriate things in the text to stimulate and challenge their efforts to read and to interpret the text. Put in another way, children select out of their experiences things they understand. If the materials are rich enough, that is, if they are complex, children at different levels of development can learn from them, and the same child can return to these materials and gain new understanding as his development proceeds.

But complexity of curriculum materials developed to serve a variety of educational objectives and a varied group of children places a heavy responsibility upon the teacher if these purposes are to be realized. For example, a text may offer material which could furnish practice in reading comprehension at several levels and practice in interpretation at several levels; it could provide an exposition, an illustration, or a problematic case from which the child could be helped to develop understanding of a concept or principle; and the understanding could be at several levels of generalization. Furthermore, the text could furnish material which would evoke the child's emotional response at several levels of appreciation. Most teachers require special training in order to use such complex materials for these several purposes. Also, for many, the problem of managing group activities, including class discussions, which effectively involve children at several levels of development, is a serious one.

One of the major causes of failure in curriculum projects has been the failure to include the teacher as a commonplace in curriculum projects and to make adequate provision for teachers to develop the interest, the understanding, the skills, and the confidence required for the effective use of the curriculum materials. This commonplace should be represented by those who are knowledgeable about the teachers to be employed in the program. It is not enough to have representatives who know about teaching in general.

The curriculum deliberations are not complete when plans and materials have been prepared. Robert Burns expressed a proverbial view when he wrote, "The best-laid plans of mice and men gang oft agley." I have seen a paper by Seymour Fox which includes a *verbatim* record of the deliberations that went on in a Hebrew University curriculum-development project. This record clearly illustrates the consideration given to the several commonplaces but it also illustrates another point. Even with the benefit of the participation of representatives of these commonplaces, occasionally the materials are inadequate. Hence, the need for tryout. In a large enterprise, such as one involving Hebrew schools throughout the nation, it is imperative that there be tryouts before large-scale use of materials. In order to plan and conduct appropriate tryouts, it is well to have an experienced evaluator involved in the deliberations. He can help in identifying the questions to be answered by the tryouts, the composition of the "bits and pieces" of materials that enable preliminary testing to be done in limited time, and the selection of groups of children that can furnish a reliable sample of the tryouts.

6

THE SCHOLAR, THE EDUCATOR AND THE CURRICULUM OF THE JEWISH SCHOOL

Seymour Fox

The conference on which this book is based, concerned with translation of the work of the scholar for classroom application by means of curriculum, quite properly concentrated most of its attention on the alternatives that scholarship offers for both the curriculum and the classroom teacher.

In the first session Professor Schwab explicated the most complex of the tasks involved in the collaboration between scholars and educators, the translation of scholarly materials into curriculum. In essence, he made a distinction between scholarship for the sake of scholarship and scholarship as a resource for education. It was our good fortune that Professors Gerson Cohen and Marvin Fox exemplified this distinction in their respective fields, Jewish history and Jewish thought.

Schwab demonstrated how scholarship viewed as a resource will generate alternative possibilities to be considered for curriculum. Such alternatives must be weighed by the participants in the group developing curriculum (the "college" as it experiences collegiality [1]) in terms of its estimates of the needs of children and teachers, and the various demands and realities of society.[2] Not only did Schwab argue this point by introducing the notion of commonplaces — the subject matter, the child, society, and the teacher — but he demonstrates in his paper how the legitimate demands of each of these commonplaces will result in a rejection of some alternatives as well as generate new and novel ones. Again, we were fortunate that Cohen and Fox, in their papers, demonstrated an awareness of the role of the commonplaces in the selection of the particular ideas of Jewish history and thought that they presented.

Even more significant is the extent to which the demands of the child, the teacher, and the society were reflected in the discussions. These demands — the "Platonic lie," [3] the problem of non-committed teachers, the variety of moral stances in the Jewish tradition [4] and their impact on teachers and students, the difficulty of sensitizing young children to moral distinctions, the concerns of the community — are some examples of the arguments presented to Schwab, Cohen, and Fox, who had undertaken to deal only with one of the commonplaces, the subject matter. I believe that this is a further demonstration of the impossibility of dealing with the commonplaces except as inseparably bound together, a fact emphasized by the discussants as they continually related the commonplaces one to another.

The conferees, while asking about the development of collegiality during the discussions, demonstrated how this communal pursuit is accomplished. When scholars and experts from a variety of fields and with diverse experiences join together to deal with a problem such as the one undertaken by this conference, they soon learn how limited they are and how dependent on the contributions of others in order to develop a curriculum group, or college.

Fortunate as we were to have had this experience together, it would be misleading to conclude that the translation from scholarship to curriculum is merely, or even essentially, an intellectual operation. The works and experience of Tyler and Schwab, and my own, have argued for curriculum as a practical endeavor.[5] By practical, we mean that no conception of Jewish history or thought, or, for that matter of any discipline, as attractive as it may be in the form presented, is viable or useful unless actual students and teachers in real classrooms can and will apply these ideas. It is certainly not useful to suggest an idea as meaningful if teachers and students do not ultimately recognize it as such. It is not feasible to recommend a conception of *paideia* as a guiding idea for the teaching of history, if the access disciplines[6] required to absorb the idea are too complex or threatening for the average teacher.

Quite the contrary, the curricular deliberation should begin with the location of the problem. By problem we mean a difficulty or failure or deprivation confronting a particular school or class. The problem may be the boredom of the teachers or students, the distortion of ideas as they are embodied in the materials, or the misunderstanding of students or misrepresentation by teachers.

The problem may be the school's inability to develop commitments and sensitivities to society's most vital interests. The problem may only reveal itself when scholars realize that history or Jewish thought as they are taught so miss the mark that the subject or its interpretation is no longer recognizable. Practical problems such as these are effective starting points for curricular deliberation.

Even if one does not accept this approach to curriculum for conceptual reasons, in practice this is what must occur. The curricular revolution of the fifties and sixties failed to grasp these realities until it was too late. Any directives derived from the academic disciplines will be filtered, modulated, popularized and distorted in the schools.

The indispensible first step taken at this conference, consideration of options for the use of scholarship in Jewish education, requires corroboration by an encounter with the realities of Jewish schools in the United States in the seventies. We must even remain open to the possibility that, as convincing as are the ideas presented at the conference, they may prove to be "impractical," or not viable for our schools at this time. Upon close scrutiny we may realize that *paideia* or the recommendation by Fox for teaching Maimonides demands knowledge, understanding, or a commitment that many teachers do not possess. The mastery of access disciplines, such as medieval history and philosophy, necessary to the understanding of the *paideia* of Andalusian Jewry, may require greater time allotments than a balanced curriculum permits.

To the questions, "Why this conference? Why *this* theoretical or quasi-theoretical discussion, when the issues are practical?", we reply with the fairly obvious. The problems we discover in our schools will be responded to by curricular materials and in-service training programs. The materials and programs will have to use scholarship as a resource. We, therefore, began our deliberations with a consideration of the translation of scholarship for curriculum purposes. For the past decade and a half the field experience of the Melton Research Center has clearly demonstrated that Jewish thought and history, or more correctly, the history of ideas, is what our students and teachers need and want. We must now take the next step: experimentation with and modification of the ideas considered at this conference in order to adapt them as guiding ideas and themes for curriculum and teaching.

We shall have to organize a curriculum group that will initially consist of psychologists, sociologists, and educators who will react to ideas presented by Gerson Cohen and Marvin

Fox. More important is the involvement from the outset of teachers who know how their peers are likely to respond to ideas and plans being developed. Teachers who join the group will be considered experts rather than typical clients. It is they who will be best able to tell us what materials are likely to enthuse teachers and enable them to elicit the interest of students. As materials are developed by the curriculum group, they must be experimented with at the earliest possible stage and in their most rudimentary form. A concept such as *paideia* should be explained to teachers and their reactions carefully noted. Through such activity we uncover possible difficulties to be encountered with the materials. The scholar must be aware of these difficulties to be able to provide the necessary introductory and supplementary information. He must observe how the additional materials are understood by the teacher, whether these actually counteract probable and typical distortions. It is at this early stage that we may discover that an idea enthusiastically adopted by the curriculum group is too complicated, or too expensive.[8] It is here that the scholar becomes aware of how many of the ideas that are obvious to him, and therefore require no articulation, represent stumbling blocks for the teacher. It is at this stage that he realizes that access disciplines such as linguistics, Bible, Talmud, general history, philosophy, etc., which he acquired in the course of his own studies, are inaccessible to the teacher.[9]

It is at this stage that the curriculum group, and especially its leader, the curriculum specialist, will hear the static interjected by teachers who have been inadequately trained and are far removed from the skills and results of Jewish scholarship. I would venture to say that what is being suggested by Cohen and Fox is so remote from the typical teacher's concept of the role and purpose of Jewish education — and more particularly the nature and function of Jewish thought and history — that many teachers will believe that they are being asked to learn and teach a *new* subject.

Our next step is then clear. We shall have to teach our materials to typical teachers as early in the process as possible for two reasons. First, to obtain a more precise reading of the teacher's understanding and of the teacher's response to the materials. And second, to be able to follow closely their suggestions for presenting the materials to students. Each of the stages — the teacher's initial reaction, the emergence of the difficulties in the material, his eventual grasp of the material, his conception of its purposes and value for students, and his notion of how it is to be taught — are invitations to distortion. The curriculum materials themselves must anticipate possible distortions.[10]

We must not forget that curricular materials, even when accompanied by intensive in-service training, are themselves a method of teacher training. The curriculum writer will be communicating conceptions of Jewish thought and Jewish history as well as suggesting ways of teaching this material. The ideas and materials have been conceived for the image of a particular student, whose favorable response and interest will be sustained by a teacher in control of and identifying with the material. If the psychologists and teachers in the curriculum group have misled us, their errors will require considerable revisions in the curriculum. A large number of curriculum materials prepared in Israel and the United States have mis-gauged the student's knowledge, skills, and motivation.

We define curriculum as a practical endeavor, because we want subject-matter specialists, psychologists, sociologists, philosophers, educators, and teachers to suggest ideas that will be applicable pedagogically within the framework of a real classroom and its problems. We believe that this will result in a more profound presentation of ideas by teachers to students and ultimately raise the levels of our schools. We know of no way of denying the teacher the leading role in the curriculum experience.

The experimentation of the Melton Research Center in the preparation of materials essentially for Jewish afternoon schools (although some materials have been adapted for and used by day schools and high schools) have impressed upon us the importance of taking great care with the steps just discussed, as well as others not here considered. The preparation of classroom materials involved the Center in in-service training, in the preparation of courses for teacher-training colleges, in summer camp programs, and in numerous lengthy exchanges with parents, rabbis, teachers, and students. These activities led us to the tentative conclusion that *being Jewish* in a free and open society means committing oneself *freely* to the Jewish tradition. The student, we learned, matures into commitment through being intellectually stimulated and affectively engaged by the traditional texts and religious observances. Thus, a school that hopes to develop true commitment to Jewish values cannot see the curriculum merely as a provider of skills and information. The school must guide the student to locate authentic Jewish ideas, make him understand how these have shaped Judaism, and how they offer him a tradition-based contemporary Jewish life style.

It follows then that the guiding concepts for curriculum in American Jewish schools should be Jewish thought and the history of authentic Jewish ideas. With this aim in mind, the Center organized the conference and heard the participants confirm the tentative assumptions growing out of the Center's practical work. We are now prepared for the next stage, the

introduction of a suggested curriculum outline based on Jewish
thought and the history of authentic Jewish ideas.

The development of a curriculum outline to guide the
preparation of materials during the coming period of the Center's
activities required a decision concerning the current structure
and time allocations of the Jewish school as it is most often
found in the United States. We are well aware that a six-hour-
a-week experience is insufficient for a Jewish education, but
because it would have been futile to create a program for non-
existing schools, we decided against planning a learning
schedule that requires fifteen to twenty hours a week. Instead,
we agreed that in order to create a desire on the part of the
community for an increase in the number of hours allocated to
Jewish education we would demonstrate the successful achievement of the six-hour school, and thus disclose the inspiring
potentialities of a greater time allotment for the appropriate
Jewish education.

We are simultaneously considering another alternative for
current experimentation. With this alternative, the six-hour week
is supplemented by the junior congregation and the youth group.
We have introduced further modification of this experiment with
a program for elite students, including supplementary and
continuing summer experiences at Camp Ramah, culminating
in a substantial period of time spent in Israel. Both alternatives
are currently being planned. In addition, the results of experiments in selected pilot schools will be exchanged for mutual
edification and practical application.

The curriculum in preparation opens by introducing the
child to Jewish education with a unit on contemporary Jewish
life, as well as a unit on *mitzvot* (Jewish practices). Both units
are meant to help the child understand himself as a member of
the Jewish people and the Jewish religious group. Both aim to

help the child discover ideas that characterize Judaism and bind the Jews of the world together. The third subject introduced to the child in his first year is Hebrew language, taught primarily as an access discipline and, secondarily, as a living language.

As an access discipline Hebrew prepares the child linguistically to study the Bible and the prayer book, the basic texts for authentic Jewish ideas. These texts and selections from rabbinic writings are treated essentially from the standpoint of Jewish thought and *paideia*. In short, the number of subjects heretofore taught in Jewish schools has been drastically reduced. Those appearing in our curriculum — Hebrew language, Bible, selections from rabbinic teaching, the prayer book, Israel, current and past Jewish history, and Jewish practice — become the vehicle by which the child will ultimately know fundamental Jewish concepts.

The curriculum proposal generated by the conference will be implemented in selected pilot schools. Concurrently, the entire project will be guided, evaluated, modified, and reformulated by the curriculum group, the college.

NOTES

1. In Chapter One Schwab describes the process of collegiality, pp. 24-29.

2. In the third conference session Rabbi Schindler (Chapter Four) articulated some of these demands most effectively.

3. The conferees debated whether the use of the "Platonic lie" or the "Platonic myth" to foster the illusion of certainty on any subject was beneficial or harmful to the child.

4. Following Marvin Fox's presentation (Chapter Three) the conferees addressed the problems of relative and absolute moral stances as these emerge in the Jewish tradition and as they affect contemporary Jewish thought.

5. Tyler, *Basic Principles of Curriculum Instruction* (Chicago: University of Chicago, 1950); Schwab, "The Practical: A Language for Curriculum" (*Schools for the 70's,* Washington D.C.: National Education Association, 1970) and "The Practical: Arts of Eclectic" (*School Review,* August 1971); Fox, "A Practical Image of the Practical" (*Curriculum Theory Network 10,* Fall 1972).

6. See Schwab, pp. 22-23; 27.

7. It will be important for us to engage in more thorough discussion of the idea of *paideia* presented by Cohen and the conception of Jewish thought presented by Fox. Such sessions will be populated by scholars and will also be served by the curriculum group so that its members can grasp fully the advantages and disadvantages implicit in these ideas. See S. Fox, "A Practical Image of the Practical," pp. 48-57.

8. The history of education is replete with examples of promising ideas and exciting programs that were abruptly discontinued, sometimes when they were on the brink of success, because of mounting costs, problems of credibility due to long periods of experimentation, and difficulties with inadequate personnel.

9. These are not insoluble problems. The chapter on theology and its interpretation prepared by Fritz Rothschild ("Teaching the Torah: An Essay

in Interpretation,'' *Genesis: The Teachers Guide,* New York: Melton Research Center, 1967) and a chapter prepared for the new high school biology program by Joseph Schwab (*High School Biology Teacher's Handbook,* New York: American Institute of Biological Sciences, 1960, 1961) are examples of how information about access disciplines can be provided in popular form.

10. An interesting example is Leonard Gardner's *Teacher's Guide for Genesis* prepared for the Melton Research Center, now being rewritten on the basis of new problems arising in the field.

BOARD OF GOVERNORS

115

ACADEMIC BOARD

GERSON D. COHEN, Chairman
> Chancellor and Jacob H. Schiff Professor in Jewish History, The Jewish Theological Seminary of America

BURTON COHEN
> Assistant Professor in Education, The Jewish Theological Seminary of America

LAWRENCE A. CREMIN
> President and Frederick A.P. Barnard Professor in Education, Teachers College, Columbia University

SYLVIA ETTENBERG
> Dean of Educational Development, The Jewish Theological Seminary of America

LOUIS FINKELSTEIN
> Chancellor Emeritus and Solomon Schechter Professor in Education, The Jewish Theological Seminary of America

MARVIN FOX
> Chairman, Department of Near Eastern and Judaic Studies and Philip W. Lown Professor of Jewish Philosophy, Brandeis University

SEYMOUR FOX
> Director, School of Education and Professor of Curriculum Theory and Research, Hebrew University, Jerusalem

AVRAHAM HOLTZ
> Simon H. Fabian Professor in Hebrew Literature, The Jewish Theological Seminary of America

DAVID LIEBER
> President and Samuel A. Fryer Professor in Bible, University of Judaism

116

JOSEPH LUKINSKY
  Chairman, Department of Education and Associate Professor in
  Education, The Jewish Theological Seminary of America
ELAINE MORRIS
  Director, Melton Research Center for Jewish Education
LOUIS NEWMAN
  Director, Bureau of Jewish Education of Boston
JOSEPH SCHWAB
  Visiting Fellow, Center for the Study of Democratic Institutions
  and Professor Emeritus of Education and Natural Sciences, Uni-
  versity of Chicago
RALPH TYLER
  Director, Center for Advanced Study in the Behavioral Sciences

PUBLICATIONS

BIBLE

Understanding Genesis by Nahum Sarna.

One-volume compendium of scholarly information about the first book of the Bible, relating history, archeology, and comparative religion, and stressing biblical religious values and ethics.

Genesis: The Teacher's Guide by Leonard Gardner and others.

A pattern of instruction for practical use in the classroom. Literary analysis of Genesis for elementary school teachers. Offers recommendations for helping students discover ideas in text.

Genesis: The Student's Guide by Louis Newman and others. Vol. I, II.

A complete text (J.P.S. translation of Genesis) with workbook exercises for classroom enquiry. Hebrew *kitzur* for afternoon schools maximizing Hebrew language skills. A series of narratives containing historical background and supplementary material in *midrash* and *halakha*.

Teacher's Supplement to Genesis: The Student's Guide by Louis Newman and others. Vol. I, II.

Answers to the workbook exercises in the Student's Guide and aids for teaching *midrash*.

A Children's Introduction to Torah by Shirley Newman.

A "read aloud" book for seven- and eight-year-olds with color illustrations. Teacher's Guide by Louis Newman. Children's Workbooks.

Adult's Guide to Genesis by Priscilla Fishman. **Leader's Guide. Participant's Guide.**

Exercises for discussions based on religious and philosophic themes in Genesis.

Understanding Exodus by Moshe Greenberg. Vol. I.

A scholar analyzes how several Israelite traditions were composed into a harmonious narrative. Inquiry into text emphasizing its religious message.

Exodus: The Teacher's Guide

Experimental edition of work in progress.

JEWISH THOUGHT

The Concept of God in Jewish Education by Fritz A. Rothschild.

Essay containing a programmatic outline for religious school instruction in theology.

Truth and Metaphor in the Bible by Fritz A. Rothschild.
Essay on interpretation.

Jewish Thought by Shirley Newman.

Highly detailed teacher's manual for teaching *midrash*. Analysis of selected Genesis *midrashim* containing ideas of universal significance. For high school students. Experimental edition.

Jewish Religion in America: Student Source Book by Shuly Schwartz and Alan Silverstein.

A collection of speeches and essays tracing the origin and development of the three main groups of American Jewry. For high school and adult education.

Jewish Religion in America: Teacher's Guide by Shuly Schwartz and Alan Silverstein.

An analysis of sources and suggested lesson plans.

HISTORY

The Birth of Classical Judaism, A Model of Historical Inquiry by Ivan G. Marcus, based on a seminar by Gerson D. Cohen.

A historian reconstructs segments of Jewish past experience from the earliest Babylonian exile (597 BCE) up to the advent of Alexander The Great (Persian Period). Intended for use in Jewish studies departments at high school and college level.

Teachers Guide by Baila Shargel.
Being developed.

The Heroes of Masada by Geraldine Rosenfield.
History of the mountain fortress and contemporary archeological discoveries and reconstruction. Illustrated booklet for junior high school readers.

PRAYER & MITZVOT

Teaching the Traditional Liturgy by Burt Jacobson.
Analysis of specific prayers; suggestions for evoking experiences related to prayer.

Outlines for first- and third-year curriculums in Jewish holidays, practices and ritual. Experimental chapters.

HEBREW LANGUAGE

Melton Biblical Hebrew Language Program
An experimental Hebrew language program designed to prepare students to study the Bible and Siddur. Includes biblical vocabulary, grammar and cultural background materials. Now in the fourth year of experimental use.

Alphon by Shlomo Haramati.
A primer designed to assist students in learning the mechanics of reading.

Mikra'ah Rishonah by Shlomo Haramati, Shlomo Skolsky, Chaim Rabin.
Reader with original stories, vocabulary lists and supplementary

readings. Graded vocabulary and grammar to develop reading comprehension skills.

Mikra'ah Shniyah by Shlomo Haramati, Shlomo Skolsky, Chaim Rabin.
Advanced reader with original stories and supplementary readings. Graded vocabulary and grammar to develop reading comprehension skills.

Audio-visual Aids posters; cassette tapes.

Teacher's Guide to the Alphon and Mikra'ah Rishonah Melton Staff.
Instructional objectives; sample lesson plans; suggested activties.

Student Workbook to the Mikra'ah Rishonah Experimental chapters available.

OTHER

The Major Curriculums for Jewish Schools: An Analysis by Walter Ackerman.
An examination and evaluation of the guiding principles inherent in the curriculums of the United Synagogue Commission on Jewish Education and the Bureaus of Jewish Education in Baltimore, Boston, Chicago, Detroit and Los Angeles.

An Annotated Bibliography of General Juvenile Literature To Be Used Within The Jewish Educational Curriculum by Judith Segal.
Fifty-four annotated items of fiction for children nine through fourteen, reflecting ethical and moral values found in Genesis.